MW00577018

# Endorsements

"Paul presents an understanding of the rapture that will challenge you. I found a well written and balanced discussion of the prevailing views concerning the timing of the rapture, with new arguments that I have not seen in my studies. Come quickly, Lord Jesus! (Rev. 22:20)."

*Bill Tobin, Professional Engineer*
**Houston, Texas**

"I have observed Paul spending year after year diligently studying the Bible to enlighten believers to truth that most will not find through their own studies. Personally, I never felt comfortable with making a decision regarding the timing of the rapture, but Paul brought up specifics of the dominant views that I had never heard from any of the well-known proponents of those views. Paul's points have forced me to conclude. I strongly recommend this book to anyone who is serious about understanding the timing of the rapture."

*Ed Cates, CEO, Consumer Products Company*
**Birmingham, Alabama**

"There are a lot of books written on 'End Times.' I've read several of them. But every once in a while, one comes along that blows a fresh wind over traditional thinking, challenging the reader to reestablish or reconsider their position. Paul did this big time in *The Timing of The Rapture*. His insights and depth of knowledge should be required reading for anyone interested in understanding the evangelical views surrounding this critical event which, while all may not agree as to its timing, all will agree as to its certainty!"

*Dick Hastings, M.Div; BCCC; CCC*
*Executive Director, Educare*
**Tuscaloosa, Alabama**

# THE TIMING
# OF THE
# RAPTURE

Paul R. Wild

The Timing of the Rapture

© Copyright 2016 Paul R. Wild

7710-T Cherry Park Drive, Suite 224
Houston, TX 77095
(281) 830-8724

http://www.WorldwidePublishingGroup.com

Printed in the United States of America

Ebook: 978-3960283553
Softcover: 978-1-365-80909-5
Hardcover: 978-1-60796-961-7

# TABLE OF CONTENTS

*A brief note on the US in Bible prophecy; a challenge to those with a laissez faire attitude toward prophetical warnings; and an invitation to study this topic from a fresh, new perspective.*

*Key terms relative to the rapture are defined to form a foundation for further study.*

*What is the Tribulation?*

*What does he do during the Tribulation?*

*The length of the Tribulation is defined to settle confusion between 7 years or 3.5 years.*

*What is the rapture?*

*The Pre-, Mid-, and Post-Tribulation rapture positions are explained.*

*The beginnning of the debate. Pre-Trib and Post-Trib positions on the significance of the Feasts of Israel, how unsaved Gentiles fit into the Tribulation and the Millennium, and the identification of those who are "taken" versus those who are "left behind."*

*The relationship of the trumpets of Joel, Matthew, 1 Corinthians, 1 Thessalonians, and Revelation to the timing of the rapture.*

*Who or what is the restrainer, and is the restrainer's absence synonymous with the rapture?*

*The idea that Christ can return at any time as an argument for a pre-Trib rapture is evaluated.*

*A quick overview of the major points is presented.*

*A brief history of the author's path to discovery regarding the rapture, plus observations on the weaknesses and strengths of the major positions, with a warning to heed prophecy.*

*A compendium of verses regarding the Day of the Lord.*

*Tools for studying the Bible that were used for writing this book.*

# PREFACE

The impetus for writing this book is based on certain phenomena I have observed over the last few years with respect to how the Body of Christ responds to prophetical warnings. A few years ago, I wrote a book entitled *Is the United States Mentioned in Bible Prophecy?* My answer was and is 180 degrees opposite of the vast majority, if not the entirety, of the major names in Bible prophecy teaching. The majority view is that the United States (US) is not mentioned specifically but, at best, peripherally through parallels to Israel and God's judgment on it. Some of the more well-known prophecy teachers are very stalwart about the majority view. From their perspective, as a nation, we are tracking right along with how the Israelites tracked before their judgment as a nation, first with the northern tribes under the Assyrians and then the southern tribes under the Babylonians, but they add that the Bible does not mention the US.

There is another view, British Israelism, propagated by the cultish Worldwide Church of God under Herbert Armstrong, that Great Britain and the US are populated by descendants of the lost 10 tribes of Israel, i.e., the northern tribes carried away into captivity by the Assyrians. These folks see certain terms in Old Testament (OT) prophecies as cryptic language for the US; but considering the source of this view, their overuse of allegory, and big stretches of imagination, I put little stock in their position. I do not deny that some strong research conducted by others indicates that descendants of the tribes, particularly Dan, inhabit Europe and the US in

1

sizeable numbers, but it breaks the rule of context to apply passages that speak directly to Israel as allegorical for the US. So, within orthodox, evangelical circles (mainly Protestant), the dominant view remains that the US is not mentioned in Bible prophecy.

I disagree. Daniel 7 uses symbolism that previously has been understood to be prophecy about the Babylonians to the Romans to the antichrist's final kingdom. I, however, believe strongly that the order of nations presented in Daniel 7 is the Anglo-American alliance; the Russians with their partners the Turks, Iranians, and Syrians; the Asians composed of China, Japan, the Koreas, and India; and finally, the antichrist's kingdom. Every day the news supports this view in light of the descent of both the US and Great Britain in military power, wealth, global influence, and morality; the ascent of Russian military might, influence, and cash reserves, plus Russia's alliance with the above-referenced, Muslim nations; and the same kind of ascent for the Asians. To list the supporting evidence is too time consuming and, for me personally, too mind-numbing. Should someone deny these truths about the state of these nations, I would respond that they are either being willfully ignorant of current affairs or stubbornly clinging to an outdated and unsupportable eschatology. Is it irritating or annoying to say that? I would respond that it works both ways, because I find it troubling that well-trained theologians ignore both modern nations and current events that match the symbols and events in Daniel 7 to a T. Prophecy is being played out before our eyes, and the majority of the Church - or at least the Western faction of it - is asleep at the wheel.

This brings up the phenomena I mentioned previously. One phenomenon is that the idea that the US is mentioned in Bible prophecy has generated little interest; and even among those who have agreed with this view, little effort is made to further the message. In short, the response to my proposed revision to the Daniel 7 interpretation has been a collective yawn. I am utterly mystified as to why. To know the playbook that describes the destruction of our country and the rise of nations leading to the antichrist and, beyond that, to the return of Christ is, in my mind, of tremendous value. After all,

**2 Peter 1:19**

*We have also a more sure word of prophecy; whereunto ye do well that ye take heed, as unto a light that shineth in a dark place, until the day dawn, and the day star arise in your hearts:*

**Proverbs 22:3**

*A prudent man foreseeth the evil, and hideth himself: but the simple pass on, and are punished.*

**Hebrews 11:7**

*By faith Noah, being warned of God of things not seen as yet, moved with fear, prepared an ark to the saving of his house; by the which he condemned the world, and became heir of the righteousness which is by faith.*

3

## Revelation 1:3

*Blessed is he that readeth, and they that hear the words of this prophecy, and keep those things which are written therein: for the time is at hand.*

The value of prophecy is, at the very least, one of informing the audience to pursue preparation. As the Apostle Peter tells us, it is like a light that illuminates the way ahead of us, presumably to help us in safe passage along the trails and trials of life. It allows us to foresee the difficulties ahead and take cover, as King Solomon informs us. Moreover, the Apostle John tells us that to read and heed prophecy is to receive a blessing. To ignore prophecy is to do so at one's own peril and to miss the blessing. Noah foresaw the day of evil; it frightened him to the point that he felt compelled to build a very big boat, and he received the blessing of a fresh start and induction into the Faith Hall of Fame. And I would add, how would it have worked for Joseph and the Egyptians had he not gathered food during the seven years of abundance before the seven years of dearth?

A second phenomenon is, as I discuss with Christians current events in light of prophecy, the not-infrequent comments from them about the rapture. The comments generally run along the lines of, "Well, I'm not going to be here anyway, since the rapture will happen before everything gets really bad. I don't plan on being here during the Tribulation." This is an interesting thought, considering millions of Christians around the world are already being severely persecuted. To a Christian being lined up for slaughter by ISIS, it seems to me that nothing in the

Tribulation could be much worse. The hope of missing all the bad stuff via the rapture would sound rather hollow, I would think, to such a Christian.

I am not alone in my observation. My friend and colleague, Mark, recently relayed to me comments from a couple of men at his Bible study group who were discussing the decaying state of the world. As they were departing to head home after the study, their concluding remarks were that the decaying state of affairs aren't really going to affect them, since they aren't going to be around here anyway by virtue of the rapture. Add to that, one of my nephews, Jordan, recently commented to me in one of our discussions, "...what I hear from my Christian friends (is), 'It doesn't matter to me. I know where I'm going.' Why did Jesus say to acknowledge the signs if Christians are just going to say, 'Oh well, I'm going to heaven'?"

My thought on these cavalier mindsets is that they probably are not perceived favorably by the Lord, given His rebuke to the religious hypocrites of His day...

### Matthew 16:1-3

*The Pharisees also with the Sadducees came, and tempting desired him that he would shew them a sign from heaven. ² He answered and said unto them, When it is evening, ye say, It will be fair weather: for the sky is red. ³ And in the morning, It will be foul weather to day: for the sky is red and lowering. O ye hypocrites, ye can discern the face of the sky;* **but can ye not discern the signs of the times?**

…and by His instructions to the followers of His day:

### Mark 13:33-37

*Take ye heed, watch and pray: for ye know not when the time is.* [34] *For the Son of Man is as a man taking a far journey, who left his house, and gave authority to his servants, and to every man his work, and commanded the porter to watch.* [35] *Watch ye therefore: for ye know not when the master of the house cometh, at even, or at midnight, or at the cockcrowing, or in the morning:* [36] *Lest coming suddenly he find you sleeping.* [37] ***And what I say unto you I say unto all, Watch.***

Judging by the content of the Lord's rebuke to the religious hypocrites and His admonition to the true believers of that time, it seems to me that we ought to be about the business of carefully watching. But as a collective, we aren't carefully watching and seem to have an endemic malaise aided and abetted by the idea that we won't be around much longer to see the horrors of the Tribulation. Nevertheless, truth is truth, so if it is true that we are raptured out of here before the Tribulation, then so be it, and I very much want it to be the case. What Christian wouldn't? Even if it is true, it still seems dangerous to me to take the laissez faire attitude that the pre-Tribulation rapture viewpoint appears to engender in the Body. Since Jesus warned of wars and rumors of wars, famines, earthquakes, etc., I think some of those things still will happen even before a pre-Tribulation rapture.

That being said, I feel that a fresh examination of the evidence for or against a pre-Tribulation rapture is warranted. It is the dominant view in Western, evangelical Christianity. If it is true that we will be gone before the antichrist is revealed, then we can revel in that knowledge and seek to bring others into the kingdom in time to be carried away to meet Jesus. But if not, then we need to rid ourselves of complacency, dig down deeper than ever into a relationship with Jesus, warn not only the lost but also the believers, and prepare for the worst. If the rapture does not occur before the Tribulation, woe to the Christian who gets caught completely off guard. Imagine the shock to the senses of such a one who suddenly realizes they have no Plan A, B, or C to deal with the coming affliction. It would be horrific enough for the prepared, since even preparation will have its limits of effectiveness against the things described in Revelation, but imagine those believers whose faculties are completely overwhelmed by the worldwide shaking. Compound it by having millions upon millions of believers in that same frame of mind. It gives some understanding to the Lord's proclamation of Luke 21:26.

### Luke 21:26

*Men's hearts failing them for fear, and for looking after those things which are coming on the earth: for the powers of heaven shall be shaken.*

7

In closing, my hope for this effort is to come to a firm, unassailable conclusion to the matter: Does the rapture occur before, in the middle of, or at the end of the Tribulation? Do we miss it, or do we go through it? I invite you to explore this issue with me.

# Chapter One
# DEFINITIONS

No. Don't even go there. If you think I'm a date setter for the rapture or the return of Christ and want to find out what date I'm setting, then don't waste your time. This topic is hard enough to deal with without setting dates, since even in certain Christian camps, folks like me are considered on the lunatic fringe, so I'm not going to set myself up as a candidate for a straightjacket fitting by setting a date. In any case, I don't have a clue for a date, but I do have a clue for the general timing of the rapture. Among Christians who have an interest in eschatology in general and the timing of the rapture specifically, the topic of the timing of the rapture and Christ's return relative to that event is hotly debated. There are three major camps - pre-Tribulation rapture, mid-Tribulation rapture, and post-Tribulation rapture – and of these three, the pre-Tribbers and post-Tribbers duke it out the most, since some folks feel that the mid-Tribbers' position is simply a modified version of the pre-Tribbers' position. In addition, there don't seem to be as many of the mid-Tribbers as there are of the other two camps, at least not by my reckoning. In any case, the hope here is to conduct a definitive, iron-clad study that makes it unequivocal for the timing of the rapture.

## A Fundamental Question

A fundamental question must first be asked and answered before we set off on this study.

# What is the Tribulation?

It is intuitive that since the timing of the rapture is juxtaposed against this event, it is necessary to understand what this event is. Moses foresaw it:

### Deuteronomy 4:29-31

*But if from thence thou shalt seek the LORD thy God, thou shalt find him, if thou seek him with all thy heart and with all thy soul. 30 When thou art in tribulation, and all these things are come upon thee, even in the latter days, if thou turn to the LORD thy God, and shalt be obedient unto his voice; 31 (For the LORD thy God is a merciful God;) he will not forsake thee, neither destroy thee, nor forget the covenant of thy fathers which he sware unto them.*

It is again referenced by Jeremiah as "Jacob's trouble."

### Jeremiah 30:7

*Alas! for that day is great, so that none is like it: it is even the time of Jacob's trouble, but he shall be saved out of it.*

In the New Testament, Mark tells us…

### Mark 13:24-27

*But in those days, after that tribulation, the sun shall be darkened, and the moon shall not give her light, 25 And the stars of heaven shall fall, and the powers that are in heaven shall be shaken.* 26 *And then shall they see the Son of man coming in the clouds with great power and glory. 27 And then shall he send his angels, and shall gather together his elect from the four winds, from the uttermost part of the earth to the uttermost part of heaven.*

Going further into God's progressive revelation, specifically in the book of Revelation…

### Revelation 7:14

*And I said unto him, Sir, thou knowest. And he said to me, These are they which came out of great tribulation, and have washed their robes, and made them white in the blood of the Lamb.*

Therefore, it is a time leading up to the Second Coming of Christ in which great trouble will engulf the whole earth. Christians and Jews will suffer the worst persecution in history but ultimately will be saved by Jesus. Jesus will provide a place of protection during the Day of the Lord – "the indignation," i.e., *His* indignation at the mistreatment of

His people - for Jews who survive the Tribulation as He returns to destroy the ungodly:

### Isaiah 26:20-21

*Come, my people, enter thou into thy chambers, and shut thy doors about thee: hide thyself as it were for a little moment, until the indignation be overpast.* [21] *For, behold, the* LORD *cometh out of his place to punish the inhabitants of the earth for their iniquity: the earth also shall disclose her blood, and shall no more cover her slain.*

We further need to define the length of time for the Tribulation. We run into a problem in that one man's Tribulation is 7 years long, and another man's Tribulation is 3.5 years long. Some define it as 7 years, and some define it as 3.5 years because of the following passage:

### Daniel 9:27

*And he shall confirm the covenant with many for one week* [of years, i.e., 7 years]: *and in the midst* [after 3.5 years] *of the week he shall cause the sacrifice and the oblation to cease* [that's when the really bad stuff starts, meaning the Tribulation], *and for the overspreading of abominations he shall make it desolate, even until the consummation, and that determined shall be poured upon the desolate.*

## A Brief Detour - The Antichrist

The discussion of the duration opens up **another** can of worms. Who is "he" in Daniel 9:27? Let's detour a bit to deal with "he," and then we'll get back to the duration of the Tribulation. To work on the "he" issue, it is better to see the context of the verse, so we might as well expand it to see the whole thing.

### Daniel 9:24-27

*Seventy weeks* [of years, i.e., 490 years] *are determined upon thy people and upon thy holy city, to finish the transgression, and to make an end of sins, and to make reconciliation for iniquity, and to bring in everlasting righteousness, and to seal up the vision and prophecy, and to anoint the most Holy. *[25]* Know therefore and understand, that from the going forth of the commandment to restore and to build Jerusalem unto the Messiah the Prince shall be seven weeks, and threescore and two weeks: the street shall be built again, and the wall, even in troublous times. *[26]* And after threescore and two weeks shall Messiah be cut off, but not for himself: and the people of the prince that shall come shall destroy the city and the sanctuary; and the end thereof shall be with a flood, and unto the end of the war desolations are determined. *[27]* And he shall confirm the covenant with many for one week: and in the midst of the week he shall cause the sacrifice and the oblation to cease, and for the*

13

*overspreading of abominations he shall make it desolate, even until the consummation, and that determined shall be poured upon the desolate.*

In verse 27, "he" is a pronoun that does not identify to whom it refers, so we must look for its antecedent. In proper grammar, the antecedent is the noun that precedes the pronoun to which it refers in the structure of the sentence or series of sentences. This is critical for understanding who "he" is in the passage above, because two noun clauses are presented before it: "Messiah the Prince" in verse 25 and "the prince that shall come" in verse 26. It is the verse 26 noun clause that immediately precedes "he" in verse 27; thus, we see that this is a reference to the antichrist, because it is he who "shall destroy the city and the sanctuary," meaning that it is he who also shall "confirm the covenant," "cause the sacrifice and oblation to cease," and "make it desolate." And what will he make desolate? Perhaps Jerusalem, perhaps all of Israel; I'm not sure. Irrespective, he will destroy the city and desecrate the sanctuary, i.e., the temple that will be built on the Temple Mount, as described in Revelation:

### Revelation 11:1-2

*And there was given me a reed like unto a rod: and the angel stood, saying, Rise, and measure the temple of God, and the altar, and them that worship therein. ² But the court which is without the temple leave out, and measure it not; for it is given unto the Gentiles: and the holy city shall they tread under foot forty and two months* [3.5 years].

This is not a critical point for our discussion, but the temple described above likely will be a small edifice much like the tabernacle in the wilderness rather than the massive edifice of Herod's temple during Christ's earthly ministry. The Greek word for the temple of Revelation 11:2 is ναοῦ (na·oo′), which signifies either a small edifice or only the inner sanctum, the Holy of Holies, versus ἱερόν (hē·e·rón), the massive temple complex built by Herod that included the inner and outer courts, plus the main temple building. Paul uses another form of the word for small temple, ναὸν (na·ón), in the following passage about the antichrist:

**2 Thessalonians 2:3-4**

*Let no man deceive you by any means: for that day shall not come, except there come a falling away first, and that man of sin be revealed, the son of perdition; 4 Who opposeth and exalteth himself above all that is called God, or that is worshipped; so that he as God sitteth in the temple* [na·ón] *of God, shewing himself that he is God.*

The Jews will not build a huge edifice again on the Temple Mount; that will be reserved for Jesus to do Himself when He returns to Jerusalem and enters gloriously through the East Gate into the millennial temple. You can read about that beginning in Ezekiel 43. He will reign there for 1,000 years

15

until Satan is released to deceive the nations again, whereupon God will destroy them and usher in the New Jerusalem as the eternal dwelling for believers. You can read about that in Revelation 20 – 22.

OK, so, we tied up some loose ends; now it's time to get back on point. Regarding the "he," of Daniel 9:27, some postulate that he is Jesus, or Messiah the Prince, because, in a sense, He did cause the sacrifice and oblation to cease because He was the perfect sacrifice that the writer of Hebrews (I believe it was Paul, owing to Peter's reference in II Peter 3:15, 16 to Paul's writings that were "hard to be understood") says nullified the old sacrificial system. Perhaps it could be argued that Jesus causes Jerusalem to become desolate as a punishment for the Jews allowing the abomination into the city. Furthermore, some could argue that Jesus made a covenant for one week (7 years) with the Jews, the first half to seek the lost sheep of the house of Israel and the second half to chastise them and then save them physically from the antichrist and spiritually from eternity in hell. We need to put this to rest and clarify that the "he" in Daniel 9:27 is definitely the antichrist and not Jesus. Points to consider on this issue:

    1. Defining "Messiah the Prince" of Daniel 9:25 as the antecedent for the "he" of Daniel 9:27 rather than "the prince that shall come" of Daniel 9:26 violates standard grammatical rules for pronouns and their antecedent nouns.

    2. Messiah the Prince" shall be "cut off," meaning physically dead and thus not a participant in the

16

earthly things that this passage describes. Spiritualizing it to say that "Messiah the Prince" is orchestrating everything unseen to the human eye violates the context of the passage and the simple, straightforward understanding that the antichrist is the bad guy doing all these bad things to Jerusalem. Spiritualizing it would be eisegesis, or reading into the text something that is not there.

3. Jesus actually did not abolish the sacrifice and oblations (Daniel 9:27) in the temple during His earthly ministry. The Romans did that in 70 A.D.

4. "...the people of the prince that shall come shall destroy the city and the sanctuary," so "he" cannot be "Messiah the Prince" because, as stated above, the Romans, not the Jews, destroyed the temple. He, the antichrist, "causes the sacrifice and oblation to cease" by his destruction of "the city and the sanctuary" and by his act of sitting in the temple to declare himself as God, as 2 Thessalonians 2:4 teaches.

## Return to the Main Discussion – Tribulation Duration

All right, now we know who "he" is, so we can get back to the main discussion on how to define the Tribulation. The tension, then, is: how long is the Tribulation, 7 years or 3.5 years? If we go back to Daniel 9:24-27, we see that 70 weeks of years are determined for God to deal directly with Daniel's people as a specific, identifiable, gathered nation. We know from written history that the Israelites through the tribes of

17

Judah, Benjamin, and remnants of the ten northern tribes (it is not true that they were all lost, but that's for a separate discussion) stayed together as a distinct people group through the Babylonian and Persian captivities, through the Seleucids, and on through the Romans. They remained as a distinct people until the Romans destroyed Jerusalem in 70 A.D., and the Jews fled to the four corners of the globe until 1948, when they were reborn as a nation. Sixty-nine of those weeks have been completed, the 69th week being completed when Jesus completed His earthly ministry, specifically when Daniel 9:26 says, "Messiah shall be cut off," meaning killed. The final week is reserved for the antichrist's covenant with Israel.

### Daniel 9:27

*And he shall confirm the covenant with many for one week* [7 years]: *and in the midst of the week he shall cause the sacrifice and the oblation to cease, and for the overspreading of abominations he shall make it desolate, even until the consummation, and that determined shall be poured upon the desolate.*

What is this covenant? It is the covenant of death described by Isaiah.

## Isaiah 28:14-18

*Wherefore hear the word of the* LORD, *ye scornful men, that rule this people which is in Jerusalem.* <sup>15</sup> *Because ye have said, We have made a covenant with death, and with hell are we at agreement; when the overflowing scourge shall pass through, it shall not come unto us: for we have made lies our refuge, and under falsehood have we hid ourselves:* <sup>16</sup> *Therefore thus saith the Lord* GOD, *Behold, I lay in Zion for a foundation a stone, a tried stone, a precious corner stone, a sure foundation*: [This could refer to the rebuilt tabernacle, or temple, referred to in Revelation 11:1,2, but 1 Peter 2:5-8 equates the stone to Jesus] *he that believeth shall not make haste.* <sup>17</sup> *Judgment also will I lay to the line, and righteousness to the plummet: and the hail shall sweep away the refuge of lies, and the waters shall overflow the hiding place.* <sup>18</sup> *And your covenant with death shall be disannulled, and your agreement with hell shall not stand; when the overflowing scourge shall pass through, then ye shall be trodden down by it.*

The terms "overflowing" and "waters shall overflow" bring to mind terms from Daniel 9:27 (overspreading of abominations) and Revelation 12:15-16, i.e., the flood from Satan's mouth, probably to be understood as the antichrist's armies that pursue Israel into the wilderness of Jordan.

Let's look at Daniel and Revelation to consider the duration of the Tribulation within this 7-year covenant-with-death period.

### Daniel 7:25

*And he shall speak great words against the most High, and shall wear out the saints of the most High, and think to change times and laws: and they shall be given into his hand until a **time and times and the dividing of time*** [reference Daniel 12:7 below, one year plus two years plus a divided year equals 3.5 years].

### Daniel 12:7; 11-12

*And I heard the man clothed in linen, which was upon the waters of the river, when he held up his right hand and his left hand unto heaven, and sware by him that liveth for ever that it shall be for a **time, times, and an half*** [reference Daniel 7:25 above, one year plus two years plus one-half year equals 3.5 years] *and when he shall have accomplished to scatter the power of the holy people, all these things shall be finished.* [11] *And from the time that the daily sacrifice shall be taken away, and the abomination that maketh desolate set up, there shall be **a thousand two hundred and ninety day*** [slightly more than 3.5 years, the extra month possibly to allow the millennial temple to be rebuilt and the priesthood re-established, per Ezekiel 40 - 46]. [12] *Blessed is he that waiteth, and cometh to the* **thousand three hundred and five and thirty days** [and again, a bit more than 3.5 years, the extra 75 days possibly to allow time for the reapportionment of the land promised to Abraham to the 12 tribes of Israel for the duration of the millennial reign of Christ, per Ezekiel 47 - 48].

## Revelation 11:2

*But the court which is without the temple leave out, and measure it not; for it is given unto the Gentiles: and the holy city shall they tread under foot* **forty and two months** [3.5 years].

## Revelation 11:3

*And I will give power unto my two witnesses, and they shall prophesy a* **thousand two hundred and threescore days** [i.e., 42 months, 3.5 years], *clothed in sackcloth.*

## Revelation 12:6

*And the woman fled into the wilderness, where she hath a place prepared of God, that they should feed her there a* **thousand two hundred and threescore days** [same as Revelation 11:3 above, 3.5 years].

**Revelation 13:5**

*And there was given unto him a mouth speaking great things and blasphemies; and power was given unto him to continue **forty and two months** [and again, 3.5 years].*

No matter how you shake it, "times, time, and the dividing of time," "a thousand two hundred and threescore days," and "forty and two months" equates to 3.5 years based on a prophetical year of 360 days per year, 12 months per year, 30 days per month. This is roughly midway between a lunar year of about 354 days and a solar year of about 365 days. I haven't studied this tidbit yet to ascertain why, but note that when Jews are being referred to in Revelation, 1,260 days is referenced, and when Gentiles are being referred to, 42 months is referenced. Perhaps it's a reminder to the elect, whether Jew or Gentile, to literally count the days for precision on the timing of the Lord's return. In any case, this 3.5-year period defines the limits of the antichrist's oppression of the Jews and his satanic stand to control the world.

The Tribulation period is thus defined as 3.5 years in duration.* From the understanding of parallels, patterns, and pre-types discussed in Appendix B, specifically that

---

* See the addendum at the end of this chapter for a discussion on the first 3.5 years of the 7-year covenant period. The 2,300 days of Daniel 8:14 and how they fit into the duration issue are also addressed.

God set patterns in the OT to guide our understanding of the NT, it is worthwhile noting that most Biblical scholars calculate the duration of Christ's earthly ministry as 3.5 years. It makes total sense: 3.5 years the first time to bring the children of Israel to their senses - at least some of them - and 3.5 years the second time to bring the children of Israel to their senses – all of them - for a total of seven years to achieve completeness.

## A Second Fundamental Question

A second fundamental question must first be asked and answered before we set off on this study.

### What is the rapture?

It is alluded to in Isaiah and Daniel.

### Isaiah 26:19

*Thy dead men shall live, together with my dead body shall they arise. Awake and sing, ye that dwell in dust: for thy dew is as the dew of herbs, and the earth shall cast out the dead.*

### Daniel 12:2

*And many of them that sleep in the dust of the earth shall awake, some to everlasting life, and some to shame and everlasting contempt.*

It is fully presented in 1 Thessalonians 4:13-17.

### 1 Thessalonians 4:13-17

*But I would not have you to be ignorant, brethren, concerning them which are asleep, that ye sorrow not, even as others which have no hope. [14] For if we believe that Jesus died and rose again, even so them also which sleep in Jesus will God bring with him. [15] For this we say unto you by the word of the Lord, that we which are alive and remain unto the coming of the Lord shall not prevent them which are asleep. [16] For the Lord himself shall descend from heaven with a shout, with the voice of the archangel, and with the trump of God: and the dead in Christ shall rise first: [17] Then we which are alive and remain shall be **caught up** [raptured] together with them in the clouds, to meet the Lord in the air: and so shall we ever be with the Lord.*

The word itself is translated from the Latin, which in turn is translated from the Greek.

Latin *rapiemur*, conjugated from the verb *rapturo*, meaning to drag off, snatch, seize, carry off – from the *Latin Vulgate Bible* used by Roman Catholics; first person plural, meaning that it is an action being done to or by the person speaking, along with others of the person's group; future tense, meaning that it is something yet to be done; indicative mood, meaning that it is something that is indicated or presented as fact; passive voice, meaning that it is something done to the person speaking by something, or Someone, other than themselves.

Greek ἁρπαγησόμεθα (har·pa·gā·só·me·tha), same meaning as above yet in Koine Greek, from the *Textus Receptus*, i.e., the "Received Text" of the Greek NT.

A parallel passage that transmits the same understanding yet without the "caught up" phrase is in 1 Corinthians.

### 1 Corinthians 15:51-53

*Behold, I shew you a mystery; We shall not all sleep, but we shall all be changed, 52 In a moment, in the twinkling of an eye, at the last trump: for the trumpet shall sound, and the dead shall be raised incorruptible, and we shall be changed. 53 For this corruptible must put on incorruption, and this mortal must put on immortality.*

So, we can take it from these two passages that the Lord Jesus will sometime in the future catch up sleeping believers, meaning those who have died in Christ, with living believers; give us new, glorified bodies; and meet Him in the clouds to be with Him forever. This is the rapture. Seems simple enough.

But it's not. Rapture is a small word that has caused a big stir in the Body of Christ relative to its timing. The issue of its timing concerns when it occurs relative to the Tribulation of Revelation. The three major positions on the timing of the rapture are the pre-Tribulation rapture (pre-Trib for short), the mid-Tribulation rapture (mid-Trib), and the post-Tribulation rapture (post-Trib). It should be obvious, based on the names of the three positions, the manner in which the respective proponents of each position define the timing of the rapture. Well, it **should** be obvious, but further work on the definitions of pre-Trib, mid-Trib, and post-Trib needs to be conducted, because it can get a bit confusing.

## The Major Positions Explained

There are variations of the definitions, and it can be particularly confusing when one man's pre-Trib rapture is another man's mid-Trib rapture. What I mean by this is that some commentators actually have the same timing for the rapture relative to the appearance of the antichrist and the appearance of Christ, but because they define the length of time for the Tribulation differently, their positions appear to diverge, one calling his position pre-Tribulation and another calling his position mid-Tribulation. As for the post-Trib position, this doesn't get mixed up with the other two positions, because one particular passage defines the timing, at least according to the post-Trib folks:

**Mark 13:24-27**

*But in those days, **after that tribulation**, the sun shall be darkened, and the moon shall not give*

26

*her light, <sup>25</sup> And the stars of heaven shall fall, and the powers that are in heaven shall be shaken. <sup>26</sup> And then shall they see the Son of man coming in the clouds with great power and glory. <sup>27</sup> And then shall he send his angels, and* **shall gather together his elect** *from the four winds, from the uttermost part of the* **earth** *to the uttermost part of* **heaven.**

The post-Tribbers interpret the elect being gathered from the four winds of earth and heaven as meaning the Church, and they say this gathering occurs "after that tribulation." It would be more accurate to define the post-Trib rapture as an "end-of-Trib" rapture, since the Tribulation will not officially be over until Jesus enters Jerusalem to set up his millennial kingdom; and the rapture will occur shortly before that event, according to the post-Tribbers. In any case, we'll stick with the term post-Trib, since it's easier to use and fits the progressive pattern of pre-, mid-, and post-.

Now, as stated before, all of these positions are relative to the Tribulation, which we defined above as 3.5 years in duration. For those of you in the reading audience holding to a 7-year Tribulation period with a mid-Trib rapture, recalibrating to a 3.5-year period would now make you a pre-Trib rapture proponent in that you believe the rapture will occur before the really, really bad stuff happens. Mid-Tribbers typically define the first half of the 7-year covenant period of Daniel 9:27 as the bad *wrath of man* half of the Tribulation, and they define the second half as the really, really bad *wrath of God* half of the Tribulation. So, then, since we've dispensed with the idea of a 7-year Tribulation period, the mid-Trib position goes away; and then it simply boils down to the pre-Tribbers versus the post-Tribbers.

Now, let's discuss the pre-Trib position. This position states that the dead in Christ and those alive in Christ will be raptured sometime before the Tribulation. Of course, there again, there is disagreement amongst these folks on how long the Tribulation is - either 3.5 years or 7 years - but either way, they believe that shortly before or immediately after the Tribulation begins the Church will be raptured and sit the Tribulation out in heaven with Jesus, thereafter to return with Him to bring the Tribulation to an end. The following list presents some of the major points that the pre-Tribbers make to assert that the Church is in heaven with Jesus during the Tribulation:

**1. The word "church" is not used in the book of Revelation between Revelation 3:22 and Revelation 22:16.** Chapters 1 to 3 address the seven churches of Asia Minor that are believed by many interpreters to represent not only the collective condition of the Church at that time in the 1st century but also collectively the Church down through time. Some see it as phases, meaning the Church was primarily like one of the seven churches at a particular "phase" in history, and others believe that the Church has had facets of all seven churches throughout history. Either way, the pre-Tribbers take the absence of the word "church" through the bulk of Revelation as a clue that the Church will be gone, with the exception of new believers who will be saved during the Tribulation; those unfortunate souls won't get with the program until after the beginning of the Tribulation, according to the Pre-Trib view. Pre-Tribbers see it as incredible and totally unexpected that John would have detailed instructions for the Church in chapters 1-3 and then be absolutely silent about the Church in the following 19 chapters if, in fact, the Church continued into the Tribulation. Pre-Tribbers believe that surely the most detailed study of Tribulation events would include an account of the Church's role in the Tribulation of Daniel's 70th week if the Church is to experience it, but they believe there is no such account. Again, this belief is based on the absence of the word "church" after Revelation 3. Furthermore, they believe that it is significant that there is an abrupt shift in thought from the Revelation 2–3 Church discussion to the 144,000 Jews from the 12 tribes of Israel in Revelation 7 and 14 and the male child, Israel (Revelation 12:1-13), so that logically the Tribulation period focuses on the nation of Israel and not the Church. Therefore, to a pre-Tribber, the only timing of the rapture that would account for this frequent mention of "church" in Revelation 1–3 and total absence of "church" until Revelation 22:16 is a pre-Trib rapture.

**2. The Tribulation is deemed the Wrath of God, and 1 Thessalonians 5:9 says, "For God hath not appointed us to wrath, but to obtain salvation by our Lord Jesus Christ..."** Pre-Tribbers believe that by not being appointed to wrath the Church is not being appointed to participate in the Tribulation. They see the entirety of the Tribulation as the wrath of God.

**3.** Jesus said in Matthew 24:44, "Therefore be ye also ready: for in such an hour as ye think not the Son of man cometh," meaning that the only timeframe in which believers would not be expecting Jesus to return would be before the Tribulation. His return is "imminent." Pre-Tribbers point out that a post-Trib viewpoint would negate this point because one could simply count up the number of days (1,260) mentioned in Revelation from the time of the antichrist's ascendancy to know when Jesus will return, but Jesus clearly implies the time of His coming will surprise believers. Pre-Tribbers believe that the only way believers will be surprised is if the rapture is pre-Trib.

**4.** Paul in 2 Thessalonians 2:1-3 was comforting the Thessalonians by saying that the antichrist would be revealed before the Day of Christ to quell the Thessalonians' misunderstanding that they had somehow entered the Tribulation, thus also comforting the Church, and assuring them (and all of us) that they (and we) would not someday face the Tribulation. Although this passage does not use the term Tribulation, many pre-Tribbers equate the Day of Christ as the Tribulation in its entirety, meaning that pre-Tribbers believe Paul was comforting the Thessalonians (and us) by telling them that they (and we) would not face the Tribulation.

**5.** The "he" in 2 Thessalonians 2:7 must be the Holy Spirit Who will restrain the advent of the antichrist until He is "taken out of the way," and since the Holy

**Spirit lives in believers, when He is removed, we are removed.** This verse is viewed as an indication that the influence of the Holy Spirit on the world through us, the Church, will be removed before the Tribulation via the rapture, thereby allowing the antichrist to arise because he will have nothing or no one to restrain him.

**6. The rapture becomes of no significance if it is post-Trib.** In other words, the pre-Tribbers ask, "What's the point of a post-Trib rapture if God miraculously preserves the Church through the Tribulation? Why wouldn't God simply preserve the Church from His wrath in the same way He did with the Israelites in the wilderness while His wrath was poured out upon Pharaoh and Egypt (Exodus 8:22; 9:4, 26; 10:23; 11:7), and then usher the Church into Christ's millennial kingdom on earth? If, as the post-Tribbers believe, the only purpose of the rapture is for living believers to avoid the Day of the Lord (Battle of Armageddon), why also resurrect sleeping (dead in Christ) believers who have already escaped the Tribulation? Also, who will re-populate the earth and build the Kingdom during Christ's millennial kingdom?" Matthew 13:41-42; 25:41 teach that the unbelievers alive at Christ's return will be judged at the end of the Tribulation and be removed from the earth, but Scripture also teaches that believers will bear children during His millennial reign and that these children will be capable of sin (Isaiah 65:20; Revelation 20:7-10). Pre-Tribbers ask, "How could this be possible if all believers on earth have been glorified through a post-Trib rapture? There would be no one left to repopulate the Gentile nations on earth."

**7. The epistles of the apostles do not contain warnings of a Tribulation for which believers must prepare.** The epistles contain warnings against false prophets, doctrinal error, ungodly living, legalism, complacency, and a host of other things, but no warnings to prepare for the events described in Revelation, so say the pre-Tribbers. They maintain that one would expect to see the mentioning in the epistles of the presence, the purpose, and the conduct of the Church in the Tribulation if a post-Trib rapture were to occur; the pre-Tribbers see none of these things.

**8. The promise of Christ's return taught in John 14:1-3 parallels 1 Thessalonians 4:13-18 and is thus an assurance that the Church will spend time in heaven with Jesus before returning to earth, whereas a post-Trib rapture would allow no meaningful time for the Church to be in heaven with Jesus before the Church returns with Him to rule and reign on the earth during His millennial kingdom. Revelation 3:10 promises that the Church will be removed prior to the Tribulation.** Pre-Tribbers believe that the phrase "keep thee from" in Revelation 3:10 means that the Church will be raptured before the Tribulation, since they believe "the hour of temptation" in the verse refers to the entire Tribulation. According to this view, the Church will be in heaven in the "mansions" prepared for us, waiting for the time to return in victory at the end of the Tribulation.

**9. The characteristics of events at Christ's post-Trib return differ from those of the rapture.** Pre-Tribbers believe that the following two points demand that the rapture occur at a time significantly different from that of Christ's return: (1) comparison of the rapture events detailed in 1 Thessalonians 4:13-18 and 1 Corinthians 15:50-58 to the events of Christ's Second Coming in Matthew 13 and 24–25 indicate several significant differences, and (2) a clear discussion of the rapture in Revelation and Matthew 24 is absent. The following table summarizes these points of difference, based on their viewpoint.

| Rapture | Return |
|---|---|
| Jesus comes in the air and returns to heaven. (1 Thessalonians 4:17) | Jesus comes to earth to rule, reign, and live among His people Israel. (Matthew 25:31-32) |
| Jesus gathers His people. (1 Thessalonians 4:16-17) | Angels gather the elect. (Matthew 24:31) |
| Jesus comes to reward. (1 Thessalonians 4:17) | Jesus comes to judge. (Matthew 25:31-46) |
| Resurrection is prominent. (1 Thessalonians 4:15-16) | Resurrection is not mentioned. (Matthew 24 – 25) |
| Believers are removed from the earth. (1 Thessalonians 4:15-17) | Unbelievers are removed from the earth. (Matthew 24:37-41) |
| Unbelievers remain on earth after the rapture. (Matthew 24:40-41) | Believers remain on earth. (Matthew 25:34). |
| There is no mention of establishing Jesus's millennial kingdom on earth (not stated in the 1 Thessalonians 4 and 1 Corinthians 15 passages, but an argument from silence). | Jesus returns to set up His millennial Kingdom on earth. (Matthew 25:31, 34) |
| Believers will receive glorified bodies. (1 Corinthians 15:51-57) | No one will receive glorified bodies (not stated in the Matthew 24-25 passages, but an argument from silence). |

| Believers are removed from unbelievers at the rapture. (1 Thessalonians 4:15-17) | In the parable of the wheat and tares, the tares (unbelievers) are removed from the midst of the wheat (believers) at Christ's return. (Matthew 13:24-30,36-41) In the parable of the dragnet, the bad fish (unbelievers) are removed from the midst of the good fish (believers) at Christ's return. (Matthew 13:47-50) |
| --- | --- |

This is no doubt not an exhaustive list of the pre-Tribbers' arguments, and it is probable that not all pre-Tribbers ascribe to all the points; but I believe it presents a pretty fair summary of their major points.

Now we can turn our attention to the post-Tribbers and attempt to give them a fair showing for their points. This position states that the dead in Christ and those alive in Christ will be raptured at the end of the Tribulation immediately before Jesus returns to the earth to defeat Satan and the antichrist and to begin His millennial reign from Jerusalem over all the earth. Of course, there again, there is disagreement amongst these folks on how long the Tribulation is - either 3.5 years or 7 years. Either way, they believe that shortly before Jesus returns, the Church will be raptured to be married to Him in view of all the inhabitants of the earth and shortly thereafter to return with Him to defeat the antichrist and his armies and take up rule in Jerusalem. The following list presents some of the major points that the post-Tribbers make to assert that the Church is on earth during the Tribulation:

1. **In the original Greek, the phrase "to meet the Lord" in 1 Thessalonians 4:17 refers to a friendly city going out to meet the visiting king and escorting him back to the city, indicating that this phrase points to a post-Trib rapture.** Post-Tribbers believe that the use of the Greek word, ἀπάντησιν (a·pán·tā·sin, i.e., "meet"), in 1 Thessalonians 4:17 has the idea of a great welcoming of the king by the citizens followed immediately by a glorious entry into the city, based on its use elsewhere in the NT, thus supporting a post-Trib rapture. Its other two uses in Matthew 25:6 and Acts 28:15 refer, respectively, to the bridegroom going forth to meet the bride who comes out to meet him and to the Roman Christians coming out to meet Paul, Luke, and the others as they came into Rome. In all cases, someone is going out to meet someone who is coming into a populated area. To the post-Tribber, this is a picture of Christ gathering the elect via the rapture immediately before entering into Jerusalem to set up His millennial kingdom.

2. **Paul writes in 1 Thessalonians 5:2,6 for believers to be alert to "the day of the Lord," indicating that believers would be around just prior to it.** Post-Tribbers say that if a pre-Trib rapture was Paul's teaching, then he would not have felt compelled to tell the Thessalonians to be alert to the "day of the Lord," which the post-Tribbers interpret as the day the Lord actually returns, not the entire Tribulation period. The only way to be alert for this specific day would be if one were still on earth to look for it.

**3. Matthew 24:37-42 and Mark 13:24-27, where people are removed from the earth and heaven "after that tribulation," teach a post-Trib rapture.** Post-Tribbers say that the people being removed are believers, and their removal doesn't occur until after all the bad things happen that Jesus discusses prior to these passages in Matthew and Mark.

**4. Revelation is addressed to the Church in Revelation 1-3, and there would be no need to do so if the Church will not experience the Tribulation of Revelation 6–19 due to a pre-Trib rapture.** Pre-Tribbers claim that God frequently warned Israel in the OT of impending judgment, even though the generation who received the prophecy would not experience it; but post-Tribbers respond that that model didn't hold true for Jeremiah and Ezekiel, both of whom prophesied and observed some of their prophecies come true. Joseph prophesied of an impending famine, and it happened in his lifetime. In any case, post-Tribbers say that pre-Tribbers miss the point that the prophecies *did* eventually happen to a generation of Israelites, so there is no reason to believe that it will be any different for the Church.

**5. A pre-Trib rapture would result in two Second Comings of Christ, while Scripture teaches only one Second Coming.** Post-Tribbers believe that Scripture nowhere teaches a partial coming of the Lord to gather the Church and then return to heaven, i.e., the return to heaven is a supposition rather than a clear statement that it actually occurs. They believe there is one Second Coming that involves gathering the Church for the whole world to see the marriage of the Bride to the Bridegroom, as presented in Revelation 19, followed immediately by their return to the earth to set up Christ's millennial kingdom.

**6. Jeremiah 30:7 says, "Alas! for that day is great, so that none is like it: it is even the time of Jacob's trouble; but he shall be saved out of it," which is the same kind of language used in Revelation 3:10, indicating that Revelation 3:10 points to a post-Trib rapture.** Post-Tribbers maintain that you cannot be saved out of something if you are not first in it, meaning in the Tribulation. This would presumably include saved Jews, i.e., Messianic Jews who had previously committed to Christ before the Tribulation.

**7. The only mention of the Church being in heaven in Revelation 4–18 is of those who were martyred, indicating that the Church has not been raptured and remains on earth during the period presented in these chapters.** In these chapters, the post-Tribbers state that the Church is identified by terms such as "brethren," "fellow servants," "saints," "martyrs," and the like, and these people are right in the thick of the Tribulation. There is no mention of the Church as a collective in heaven apart from those who were martyred during the Tribulation. You can see this in the believers slain for their testimony during the Tribulation and shown under the altar in Revelation

6:9, and in Revelation 7:9-17, where the martyred believers are given white robes because they "washed their robes, and made them white in the blood of the Lamb." (v. 14)

**8. The chronological sequence of 1 Thessalonians 4:13-17 and 1 Thessalonians 5:1-9 teach a post-Trib rapture, since the Day of the Lord mentioned in 1 Thessalonians 5:2 occurs at the end of Daniel's 70th week (Daniel 9:24-27).** The gathering of the believers in 1 Thessalonians 4:15-17 at the "**coming** of the Lord" is viewed as the same time as when "the day of the Lord so **cometh**" in 1 Thessalonians 5:2; and the Day of the Lord is viewed as the Lord's return at the end of Daniel's 70th week (of years). Daniel 7:25-27 and 11:45 teach that the end of the week will result in the destruction of the antichrist and the establishment of Christ's dominion.

**9. The rapture trumpets of 1 Thessalonians 4:17 and 1 Corinthians 15:52 and the trumpets of Joel 2:1, Matthew 24:31, and Revelation 11:15 coincide and thus contradict a pre-Trib rapture, since the trumpet of Matthew 24:31 clearly is after the horrific events described by Jesus in Matthew 24, those events being defined by Jesus as the "tribulation" in Matthew 24:21.** The post-Tribbers state that all these trumpets line up in time at the end of the Tribulation, such that the trumpets associated with the rapture of the Church in 1 Thessalonians and 1 Corinthians are also the same trumpets (or trumpet) that herald the Day of the Lord

(Joel 2:1), the gathering of the elect (Matthew 24:31) after the Tribulation (Matthew 24:21), and the world becoming the kingdom of Christ (Revelation 11:15).

**10. The promise of deliverance for the Church in 2 Thessalonians 1:6-10 when Jesus returns to judge the world points to a timing of the rapture to be later than a pre-Trib rapture, indicating a post-Trib rapture.** The deliverance of the Church, or the "rest with us" in v. 7, is seen as occurring when the Lord comes in "flaming fire taking vengeance" in v. 8, when "he shall come to be glorified in his saints" in v. 10. The rapture results in our rest, and that rest is concurrent with Christ's return.

**11. The Church participates in the first resurrection, and since the first resurrection is described in Revelation 20:4-6, this points to a post-Trib resurrection, and this resurrection is the same as the rapture.** Post-Tribbers point out that a resurrection is not the same as a revivification (or resuscitation). Lazarus was revivified but only into his natural, earthly body. The resurrection is not only coming back to life but also coming back to life into a glorified, spiritual body, i.e., one which is eternal and does not decay. There is only one resurrection taught in Scripture, meaning all other instances of people coming back to life in Scripture were revivifications only. The rapture is clearly taught as an event that results in the individual members of the Body of Christ receiving glorified bodies, meaning a resurrection.

40

This resurrection is discussed by Paul in 1 Corinthians 15, the same chapter that forms the context for his discussion of the rapture in verses 51 to 53, meaning the resurrection and the rapture are one and the same thing. This resurrection is taught in Revelation 20:4-6 as an event after the events of Revelation 4-18, and it is reserved only for the "blessed and holy" (v. 6), including those who "had not worshipped the beast, neither his image, neither had received his mark," (v. 4) meaning Christians who go through the Tribulation.

**12. In Matthew 10:22; 24:13 and Mark 13:13, Jesus says, "…he that endureth to the end shall be saved," the admonition being to hang on until the end, not until a mysterious, unseen, partial visitation by the Lord to gather up believers before the end.** Post-Tribbers maintain that the Lord was teaching us to hang on until His return at the end of the Tribulation. The "end" is what Daniel speaks of as "at the **time** appointed the **end**," "the **time** of the **end** shall be the vision," "the last **end** of the **indignation**," and "the **time** of the **end**" in Daniel 8:17,19; 11:35,40; 12:4,9. All of these verses refer to the time leading up to the return of Christ. As stated previously for Isaiah 26:20, the "indignation" is Christ's indignation at the mistreatment of His people, which will result in the destruction of the pagans on the Day of the Lord.

**13. Paul's assertion that, "God hath not appointed us to wrath, but to obtain salvation by our Lord Jesus Christ" in 1 Thessalonians 5:9 should not be**

construed as descriptive of the entire Tribulation period but only to the "day of the Lord," which is described directly or indirectly in at least 48 passages of Scripture. Only a few of the verses are presented below so as to not greatly bog down the discussion; the entirety of the passages is presented in Appendix A.

1.  Job 21:30

*That the wicked is reserved to the **day of destruction**? they shall be brought forth to the **day of wrath**.*

2.  Isaiah 2:12

*For the **day of the Lord** of hosts shall be upon every one that is proud and lofty, and upon every one that is lifted up; and he shall be brought low:*

3.  Jeremiah 46:10

*For this is the **day of the Lord God** of hosts, a **day of vengeance**, that he may avenge him of his adversaries: and the sword shall devour, and it shall be satiate and made drunk with their blood: for the Lord GOD of hosts hath a sacrifice in the north country by the river Euphrates.*

4.  Joel 1:15

*Alas for the day! for the **day of the Lord** is at hand, and as a destruction from the Almighty shall it come.*

5. Joel 3:14

*Multitudes, multitudes in the valley of decision: for the **day of the Lord** is near in the valley of decision.*


6. 1 Thessalonians 5:2

*For yourselves know perfectly that the **day of the Lord** so cometh as a thief in the night.*


7. Revelation 6:17

*For the great **day of his wrath** is come; and who shall be able to stand?*


If we were to conduct intensive studies of the phrases "at that time" and "in that day," it is conceivable that several dozen other references to the Day of the Lord might be found, but sufficient for now are the ones referenced herein.

The post-Tribbers believe the Day of the Lord needs to be understood as an actual, singular day, not a long period of years. They protest against those who believe that the Tribulation and the Day of the Lord are one and the same, saying that if that were the case, it would contradict the contexts of these passages where "day" is used. As an example, if Elijah is to come before the "great and terrible day of the Lord," (Malachi 4:5), and if Elijah is to be equated to one of the two faithful witnesses of Revelation 11:3, and if Elijah is witnessing *during* the Tribulation, then the Day of the Lord must come at the end of the Tribulation. This means that the "day of the Lord" really is a day and not a lengthy period of 3.5 to 7 years. That being said, the post-Tribbers state that 1

Thessalonians 5:9 teaches that believers will be preserved from experiencing that one day but not the entirety of the Tribulation.

Post-Tribbers state that it is helpful to understand the difference between judgment and wrath. They believe the earth's inhabitants will be judged during the Tribulation, meaning punishment, but not to a complete end of the earth as we know it. By the post-Tribbers' reckoning, the punishments, or judgments, will still allow people to repent, and some of them will repent, in some part aided by the witness of the 144,000 sealed Jews functioning as global evangelists. Within the confines of the Tribulation descriptions from Revelation 6 to 19, Revelation uses the words "judgment" or "judgements" six times, and the contexts have to do with the idea of revealing something about God to people on earth, allowing them to make decisions, leading either to a blessing or a cursing. The elect, either as Christians entering the Tribulation or as those who become Christians during the Tribulation, directly or indirectly will have to endure these judgments. Post-Tribbers say the wrath of God revealed during the Day of the Lord is an entirely different animal. They maintain that this is the one day to which the elect have not been "appointed," but it's too late for the pagans, at that point. No turning back. God provides no more time for repentance, no restraint in His destruction of the godless, no hesitation, no delay, and utter annihilation of the current world system.

In the same manner as for the pre-Tribbers, this is not an exhaustive list and likely not one that is in accord with all Post-Tribbers' views, but it should give a reasonable idea of the post-Tribbers' major points.

## DEFINITIONS Addendum

### The First Half of the 7-Year Covenant Period

If the Tribulation is only 3.5 years in duration during the latter half of the 7-year covenant period, then what occurs during the first half of that period? Great question, and I can offer only speculation as an answer. If we can recognize that the cryptic, apocalyptic, phantasmagorical language of Revelation will have actual, real-world equivalents in the future, then we can apply that understanding to making reasonable assumptions about the first half of the 7-year period. What I mean by this is that the over-the-top descriptions of the events in Revelation will actually occur within the context of the normal geopolitical and social movements that have been occurring for millennia. Politicians make promises, governments make treaties, countries make war with one another, currencies fluctuate, and financial depressions cycle in and out. That being said, one can imagine that after the antichrist makes a covenant with Israel that allows the tabernacle to be rebuilt on the Temple Mount and the daily sacrifices to commence, there must be a post-treaty-signing period where construction of the tabernacle must occur, the priests must be purified for service, the sacrificial animals must be procured, and so on. There will be an administrative side to the covenant where normal administrative things have to be done. There may be United Nations observers doing the normal, useless things that they do now. It is likely during this time that the antichrist will be consolidating power, making deals with the ten kings that Daniel 7:24 and Revelation 17:12 say will serve him.

I postulated in my book, *Is the United States Mentioned in Bible Prophecy?*, that the antichrist will explode onto the world scene after the wars of Psalm 83 and Ezekiel 38 and 39, during the aftermath when the whole world will be in a state of panic and chaos. I believe these wars are pre-Tribulation wars wherein Israel will be attacked, but the Russian and Muslim invaders will be wiped out, leaving a power vacuum into which the antichrist will step to convince the world that Israel is special and deserves its own temple, and that he is the only guy who can solve the "controversy of Zion." (Isaiah 34:8) Even now, there are prophecy ministries who feel, as I do, that the global elitists are using the Russians and Muslims to stir up trouble to the point that they foolishly will attack Israel, knowing that the invaders will be destroyed. The elitists want them out of the way, knowing that they are uncontrollable and will never follow the elitists' agenda. After the dust settles and the antichrist is ensconced as the global leader, financial markets will recover, trade and commerce will increase, and the global religious system headquartered in the place where all the pantheistic, pagan religions started under Nimrod – Babylon, i.e. modern-day Iraq – will be established. Zechariah 5:11 says Babylon will be rebuilt; the UN currently is developing plans for this. (No, Rome is not the Babylon of Revelation. Babylon means Babylon.)

While Babylon is being rebuilt, the antichrist will be building his army, not only military personnel but also true believers who believe he is the solution to the world's problems. Like his father, Satan, he delusionally will believe his own press and exalt himself in his own warped, perverse mind to think that he is the Christ; in fact, Scripture teaches us that his dad will enter into and possess him to enable him to be that delusional. Like father, like son. The build-up of

46

his coalition and his self-delusion will cause him to think himself to be God, emboldening him to enter into the Holy of Holies to declare himself to be God. That act will initiate the latter half of the 7-year covenant period, otherwise known as the Tribulation.

And so, I conclude my speculation about the first half of the "covenant with death, the agreement with hell." I welcome others to take a crack at it.

## The 2,300 Days of Daniel 8:14

### Daniel 8:13-14

*Then I heard one saint speaking, and another saint said unto that certain saint which spake, How long shall be the vision concerning the daily sacrifice, and the transgression of desolation, to give both the sanctuary and the host to be trodden under foot? ¹⁴ And he said unto me, Unto two thousand and three hundred days; then shall the sanctuary be cleansed.*

The context of this verse is the antichrist and his defilement of the temple of Revelation 11:1-2, which will be the small tabernacle built during the 7-year covenant period of Daniel 9:27. The antichrist will cause the daily sacrifice to cease during this period. The daily sacrifice is composed of the evening and morning sacrifices referenced in Numbers 28:2-4.

### Numbers 28:2-4

*Command the children of Israel, and say unto them, My offering, and my bread for my sacrifices made by fire, for a sweet savour unto me, shall ye observe to offer unto me in their due season.* ³ *And thou shalt say unto them, This is the offering made by fire which ye shall offer unto the LORD; two lambs of the first year without spot day by day, for a continual burnt offering.* ⁴ *The one lamb shalt thou offer in the morning, and the other lamb shalt thou offer at even;*

Daniel confirms that the evening and morning sacrifices are included within the "daily sacrifice."

### Daniel 8:26

*And the vision of the evening and the morning which was told is true: wherefore shut thou up the vision; for it shall be for many days.*

The difficulty of the 2,300 days is that it does not line up with the other duration citations in Daniel and Revelation. Seven years at 360 days per year according to the Bible's prophetical calendar equals 2,520 days. Another possibility that some scholars postulate is that the 2,300 days should be cut in half, meaning the 2,300 should be understood to mean 2,300 total, cumulative morning and evening sacrifices covering 1,150 days. There is support for this view within the original Hebrew of Daniel 8:14 in that the verbiage literally says "mornings evenings" (boqer ereb), which the KJV translators interpreted as days. Well, the cutting in half doesn't quite work, either, in that it doesn't line up with the 1,260 days of a 3.5-year Tribulation.

It is important to not get lost within the two positions. Since 2,300 and 1,150 are subsets of the 7-year covenant with death and 3.5-year Tribulation periods, respectively, Daniel 8:14 does not nullify the crux of the argument that the Tribulation itself is 3.5 years in duration. Perhaps the 1,150 days is the correct number and may represent the period that "both the sanctuary and the host [will] be trodden under foot" after the antichrist walks into the temple and declares himself to be God at the mid-point of the 7-year covenant period. The 110-day period between the 1,260 days of the 3.5-year Tribulation period and the 1,150 days may be the time necessary to bring his military forces into Jerusalem to establish his administration. Perhaps the phrase "then shall the sanctuary be cleansed" means that at the end of the 1,150 days, Jesus will return through the East Gate (Ezekiel 43:1) to purify and sanctify the Temple Mount. However, I concede that 2,300 literal days may also be the correct interpretation and may represent the time it takes from the initiation of the daily sacrifices within the larger 7-year, 2,520-day covenant period until Christ's return. It might be that the 220-day period between 2,520 days and 2,300 days allows for the building of the tabernacle, initiation of the priests, and beginning the daily sacrifices. Hopefully, time and additional research will solve this puzzle.

# Chapter Two
# POINT – COUNTERPOINT

All right, so, now we have arrived at the point where we want to make a fresh attack on the problem. We need to begin discussing the points and counterpoints made by the proponents of each position to see which group has the winning argument for each point. Not every point that each camp has will be addressed, but enough of the major points will be addressed to be able to come to a firm conclusion. It is not necessary to cover every point, since Scripture does not contradict itself, which means that reaching definitive conclusions on the major ones locks the other, lesser points in place with respect to proper interpretation. During our analysis, we will be using the rules explained in Appendix B, should anyone care to investigate them.

The major points we will cover are the feasts of Israel, the timing of the last trumpet announcing the rapture, the imminence of the rapture, and the restrainer of the rapture.

One of the rules from Appendix B we will use is that God uses a physical reality to model a spiritual reality. Understanding this makes it easier to understand the timing of the rapture. From my perspective, the first physical reality to examine must be the feasts, festivals, and high holy days of Israel. The basis of my argument is that Jesus and the apostles referred to them often, and it was clear that they believed Christ's earthly ministry was a fulfillment of the feasts of Israel. Borrowing from my book, *Submission*, the following is a synopsis of them:

51

We see both a *pattern* and a *pre-type* in the Seven Feasts of Israel. These are physical events that pattern and foretell the spiritual ministry of Christ.

**<u>Spring</u>** – In the spring, representing the birth of the Church, we have:

1. Passover
2. Unleavened Bread
3. Firstfruits

For Passover and Unleavened Bread, Paul tells us to clean out "the old leaven, for even Christ our passover is sacrificed for us." (1 Corinthians 5:7) We are then informed that Firstfruits represents "Christ risen from the dead, and become the firstfruits of them that slept." (1 Corinthians 15:20)

**<u>Summer</u>\*** – The summertime growth of the Church is:

---

\*This is under the current Israeli calendar that defines summer as roughly late March to the 1st of October. Historically, it was considered a late spring feast.

4. Pentecost

At Pentecost, the first believers in Acts 2 added many to their numbers under the unction of the wind and fire of the Holy Spirit.

**Fall** – In the fall, upon Christ's return, the Church has matured and is ready for harvest, thus:

5. Trumpets

6. Day of Atonement

7. Tabernacles

Trumpets will call for a Holy Convocation, a Sacred Assembly, a Harvest - "The Rapture." (Matthew 24:31; 1 Corinthians 15:52; Revelation 14:14-16) The remnant of Israel at the end of the Great Tribulation when Christ appears in the sky for all to see will mourn during the Day of Atonement, where they "shall look upon me whom they have pierced, and they shall mourn for him, as one mourneth for his only son, and shall be in bitterness for him, as one that is in bitterness for his firstborn." (Zechariah 12:10) Finally, after Jesus vanquishes His enemies and enters Jerusalem to set up His millennial kingdom, we will all celebrate Tabernacles, when our Beloved Lord will declare, "My tabernacle also shall be with them: yea, I will be

their God, and they shall be my people."
(Ezekiel 37:27) And after the millennial
kingdom, He will tabernacle with His people
for all eternity in the New Jerusalem. Yes, even
"the tabernacle of God [will be] with men, and
he will dwell with them, and they shall be his
people, and God himself shall be with them,
and be their God." (Revelation 21:3) And there
is a cyclical pattern within this pattern. God has
a tendency to re-visit something to close the
circle, to bring completion. We see this in
Tabernacles. Many scholars believe Jesus was
actually born in a September/October
timeframe, which coincides with Tabernacles
on the Jewish calendar. Jesus fulfilled
Tabernacles once at His First Advent:


**John 1:14**

*And the Word was made flesh, and dwelt*
[tabernacled] *among us, (and we beheld his*
*glory, the glory as of the only begotten of the*
*Father,) full of grace and truth.*


And He will fulfill Tabernacles again at His
Second Advent.


It is instructive to note that Jesus fulfilled Feasts 1 to 4 in
exactly the same timeframe as laid down by God in Leviticus
23. Passover is the 14th of Nissan (March/April timeframe);

Unleavened Bread is the 15th of Nissan, which can also be presented as Christ, our unleavened Bread of Life, being broken on the cross; Firstfruits is the 16th of Nissan (some commentators prefer the 17th, based on the Jewish reckoning of evenings as the beginning of a day rather than mornings – but that's for another discussion); and Pentecost is 50 days after Firstfruits in Sivan (May/June).

Trumpets is the 1st day of Tishri (September/October); the Day of Atonement is the 10th day of Tishri; and Tabernacles begins on the 15th day of Tishri. It is at this point that pre-Tribbers and post-Tribbers depart from one another. The pre-Tribbers would say that there is a significant time gap on the order of several years between Trumpets (the rapture) and the last two feasts (the return). The post-Tribbers would argue the opposite, that they come in quick succession, just as the first four feasts did during Christ's earthly ministry and its immediate aftermath.

There is more to be said about Trumpets. Trumpets is also coincident with Rosh Hashanah, the "Head of the Year," meaning the beginning of the Jewish civil year; it is also called Yom Teruah, meaning "day of shouting/blasting/blowing," depending on who you're talking to. Scholars are generally in agreement that there is not much said in Scripture about Trumpets with respect to its meaning, application, and history of celebration. However, I think we can deduce some things about it by carefully examining its institutional language:

## Leviticus 23:23-25

*And the LORD spake unto Moses, saying, [24] Speak unto the children of Israel, saying, In the seventh month, in the first day of the month, shall ye have a sabbath, a memorial of blowing of trumpets, an holy convocation. [25] Ye shall do no servile work therein: but ye shall offer an offering made by fire unto the LORD.*

It is a day of memorial and gathering. A memorial of what for a gathering of whom? Is there anything we can find in Israel's history prior to the institution of Trumpets where they blew trumpets and gathered together? Yes.

## Exodus 19:9-20

*And the LORD said unto Moses, Lo, I come unto thee in a thick cloud, that the people may hear when I speak with thee, and believe thee for ever. And Moses told the words of the people unto the LORD. [10] And the LORD said unto Moses, Go unto the people, and sanctify them to day and to morrow, and let them wash their clothes, [11] And be ready against the third day: for the third day the LORD will come down in the sight of all the people upon mount Sinai. [12] And thou shalt set bounds unto the people round about, saying, Take heed to yourselves, that ye go not up into the mount, or touch the border of it: whosoever toucheth the mount shall be surely put to death:*

*¹³ There shall not an hand touch it, but he shall surely be stoned, or shot through; whether it be beast or man, it shall not live: when the trumpet soundeth long, they shall come up to the mount. ¹⁴ And Moses went down from the mount unto the people, and sanctified the people; and they washed their clothes. ¹⁵ And he said unto the people, Be ready against the third day: come not at your wives. ¹⁶ And it came to pass on the third day in the morning, that there were thunders and lightnings, and a thick cloud upon the mount, and the voice of the trumpet exceeding loud; so that all the people that was in the camp trembled. ¹⁷ And Moses brought forth the people out of the camp to meet with God; and they stood at the nether part of the mount. ¹⁸ And mount Sinai was altogether on a smoke, because the LORD descended upon it in fire: and the smoke thereof ascended as the smoke of a furnace, and the whole mount quaked greatly. ¹⁹ And when the voice of the trumpet sounded long, and waxed louder and louder, Moses spake, and God answered him by a voice. ²⁰ And the LORD came down upon mount Sinai, on the top of the mount: [a cloudy one, verses 9 and 16] and the LORD called Moses up to the top of the mount; and Moses went up.*

There appears to be a pattern familiar to us. All right, well, let's see:

1. The Lord descends in a cloud, verses 9, 16, and 20.
   - Acts 2:9-11: The angels told the disciples Jesus will return the way He left, specifically, in a cloud.
   - 1 Thessalonians 4:17: The Lord will be waiting for us in the clouds.
   - Revelation 4:17: He comes in the clouds.

2. The people washed their clothes and purified themselves, verse 10.
   - Daniel 12:10: God's people are purified and made white during the time of the end.
   - Revelation 19:7-8: The Bride makes herself ready and is clothed in white robes.

3. A trumpet is blown, verse 16.
   - 1 Corinthians 15:52: A trumpet will accompany Christ's descent.
   - 1 Thessalonians 4:16: A trumpet is blown.

4. The people are brought forth to meet God, verse 17.
   - 1 Thessalonians 4:16-17: All believers are brought forth to meet the Lord.

You don't have to be a rocket scientist to see the parallels. Trumpets commemorates this event. Trumpets calls for a holy convocation, a gathering of God's people to meet Him. There are, of course, some differences between Israel's meeting with the Lord in Exodus 19 and our future meeting with Him. The perfect atonement necessary to perfectly cleanse Israel to be able to meet Him directly had not occurred, but that will not be the case for all believers, either asleep or alive, when He returns - He has "washed us from our sins in his own blood." (Revelation 1:5)

Beginning with Trumpets, the ten-day period leading to Atonement is referred to by the Jews as "The Days of Awe." It is a period of solemn introspection and genuflection, a period of recognition of one's sinfulness and need for redemption. It is also a time of great joy in consideration of God's mercy and love toward His people. At the end of the ten-day period on the Day of Atonement, it is recognition of God's judgment, whether one is truly penitent and deemed worthy of forgiveness and continued blessing or unrepentant, rebellious, and deserving of death and cursing.

So, where to begin? We saw earlier in the section covering the major positions that God used the feasts of Israel in the NT as markers to authenticate the ministry of Jesus. We saw that His earthly ministry fulfilled the meanings of the first four feasts of Israel, namely Passover, Unleavened Bread, Firstfruits, and Pentecost. He completed them in exactly the way they occur on the calendar within the same year. It begs the question, "Will He do so for the last three feasts in the same calendar year?"

As mentioned previously, the pre-Tribbers argue that strict adherence to the calendar order of the feasts as an indicator of the rapture's timing would violate the imminence principle that it could happen at any time:

## Matthew 24:36

*But of that day and hour knoweth no man, no, not*
*the angels of heaven, but my Father only.*

The post-Tribbers state that the argument that we cannot know the timing of the rapture based on this verse is too easily and flippantly offered without serious consideration of the verse. Jesus was in His human form when He stated that, and His knowledge was limited to only what the Father revealed to Him. It is ludicrous to think that Jesus in His glorified, heavenly state does not know when He will return for His Bride. After all, it was He who revealed to John the events of Revelation, such events including the rapture presented as the first of the two sickle harvests of Revelation 14:14-20. When He spoke of the rapture in Matthew 24:36, He spoke in the present tense at that time in history; He did not use the future tense, so it doesn't follow proper exegesis to apply a future sense of understanding to something He stated as true for that time in the past. The issue of imminence is addressed more fully in a later chapter.

The pre-Tribbers would also argue that the seemingly all-inclusive terms in Revelation that demarcate the believers from unbelievers preclude the literal calendar concept. They argue that if all believers are raptured at the end of the Tribulation, and if all unbelievers are destroyed at the Battle of Armageddon, then who is left to repopulate the earth during the millennial reign of Christ?

The post-Tribbers' answer to their argument is that there will be unbelievers during the Tribulation who do not take the mark of the beast, survive the Tribulation, and also become believers after the rapture but before Christ returns to earth. Proof of this is that the Jews will not believe in the antichrist after he sets himself up as God in the temple. The Jews will flee to the Jordanian wilderness and will not recognize Jesus as their Messiah until the Day of Atonement, where they will mourn, as Zechariah 12:10 states, because of their failure to recognize Him before that time and their recognition of their own sinfulness. That was the purpose of the Day of Atonement - to "afflict their souls" (Leviticus 23:27-32) to the point of repentance, and to atone for their sins through personal recognition of their sinfulness and need for God's forgiveness.

But there will be Gentiles who experience a similar fate. Proof of this follows:

### Isaiah 14:1-3

*For the LORD will have mercy on Jacob, and will yet choose Israel, and set them in their own land: and the **strangers** [Gentiles] shall be joined with them [the Jews], and they [Gentiles] shall cleave to the house of Jacob. ² And the **people** [Gentiles] shall take them, [the Jews] and bring them to their place: and the house of Israel shall possess them [Gentiles] in the land of the LORD for servants and handmaids: and they [the Jews] shall take them [Gentiles] captives, whose captives they were; and they [the Jews] shall rule over their oppressors [Gentiles]. ³ And it shall come to pass in the day that the LORD shall give thee rest from thy sorrow, and from thy fear, and* *from the hard bondage wherein thou wast made to serve,*

## Isaiah 60:1-5

*Arise, shine; for thy light is come, and the glory of the LORD is risen upon thee. ² For, behold, the darkness shall cover the earth, and gross darkness the people: but the LORD shall arise upon thee, and his glory shall be seen upon thee. ³ And the Gentiles shall come to thy light, and kings to the brightness of thy rising. ⁴ Lift up thine eyes round about, and see: all they gather themselves together, they [Gentiles] come to thee: thy sons shall come from far, and thy daughters shall be nursed at thy side. ⁵ Then thou shalt see, and flow together, and thine heart shall fear, and be enlarged; because the abundance of the sea [of Gentiles] shall be converted unto thee, the forces of the Gentiles shall come unto thee.*

## Jeremiah 16:19-21

*O LORD, my strength, and my fortress, and my refuge in the day of affliction, the Gentiles shall come unto thee from the ends of the earth, and shall say, Surely our fathers have inherited lies, vanity, and things wherein there is no profit. ²⁰ Shall a man make gods unto himself, and they are no gods? ²¹ Therefore, behold, I will this once cause them to know, I will cause them [Gentiles]*

*to know mine hand and my might; and they*
[Gentiles] *shall know that my name is The LORD.*


There are numerous other passages that support the idea that Gentiles will survive the Tribulation and remain to repopulate the earth during the millennial reign of Christ. Gentiles shall serve and bless the Jews. This can only mean that certain Gentiles miss the rapture but don't miss Jesus during the 5-day period between the Day of Atonement, His descent to earth to destroy the antichrist and his armies, and the setting up of His earthly kingdom beginning with Tabernacles. Perhaps their hearts will be prepared during the Days of Awe, as they consider why the earth has been undergoing cataclysmic upheaval the prior three and one-half years, followed by the sudden disappearance of millions of those pesky Christians.

In contrast to these elect Gentiles, it is probable that in the immediate aftermath of the rapture, the antichrist and his followers will begin their foolish chant of "peace and safety" from 1 Thessalonians 5:3, as they rejoice that they finally are rid of the Christians. Jesus informs us in Matthew 24:38 that their revelry will match the hedonistic behavior of the lost souls in Noah's time. During the Days of Awe, there will be ample time for the people remaining on earth to either recognize their need for salvation or, in the case of the beast and those taking his mark, to prepare for war against the returning Lord of Glory. On Atonement, decisions will be made, either repentance for the elect Jews and Gentiles or defiance from the hedonistic, ungodly followers of the antichrist. Sometime during the timeframe between Atonement and Tabernacles, these pagans suddenly will be "taken" to the Valley of Megiddo for the great supper at the winepress of the wrath of God (the Day of the Lord), as Jesus foretold.

### Luke 13:33-37

*Whosoever shall seek to save his life shall lose it; and whosoever shall lose his life shall preserve it. *<sup>34</sup>* I tell you, in that night there shall be two men in one bed; the one shall be **taken**, and the other shall be left. *<sup>35</sup>* Two women shall be grinding together; the one shall be **taken**, and the other left. *<sup>36</sup>* Two men shall be in the field; the one shall be **taken**, and the other left. *<sup>37</sup>* And they answered and said unto him, Where, Lord? And he said unto them, Wheresoever the body is, thither will the **eagles** [fowls] be gathered together.*

### Revelation 14:19

*And the angel thrust in his sickle into the earth, and gathered the vine of the earth, and cast it into the great winepress of the wrath of God. And I saw an angel standing in the sun; and he cried with a loud voice, saying to all the **fowls** that fly in the midst of heaven, Come and gather yourselves together unto the supper of the great God.*

### Revelation 19:17

*And I saw an angel standing in the sun; and he cried with a loud voice, saying to all the **fowls** that fly in the midst of heaven, Come and gather yourselves together unto the supper of the great God;*

Recall that the Day of Atonement will coincide with Zechariah 12:10, where Jesus *will be seen* as the one whose hands they pierced. Jesus will be seen not only by the Jews but by the entire world, including those remote Gentiles who did not take the mark of the beast:

### Zechariah 12:7-11

*The LORD also shall save the tents of Judah first, that the glory of the house of David and the glory of the inhabitants of Jerusalem do not magnify themselves against Judah. ⁸ In that day shall the LORD defend the inhabitants of Jerusalem; and he that is feeble among them at that day shall be as David; and the house of David shall be as God, as the angel of the LORD before them. ⁹ And it shall come to pass in that day, that I will seek to destroy all the nations that come against Jerusalem. ¹⁰ And I will pour upon the house of David, and upon the inhabitants of Jerusalem, the spirit of grace and of supplications: **and they shall look upon me whom they have pierced**, and they shall mourn for him, as one mourneth for his only* son, and shall be in bitterness for him, as one that is in bitterness for his firstborn. [11] In that day shall there be a great mourning in Jerusalem, as the mourning of Hadadrimmon in the valley of Megiddon. [Wow. Connect the timing of this event to the mention of Megiddon, or the Armageddon of Revelation 16:16.]

## Matthew 24:27-31

For as the **lightning cometh out of the east, and shineth even unto the west;** so shall also the coming of the Son of man be. [lightning is very visible] [28] For wheresoever the carcase is, there will the **eagles** [the fowls of Revelation 14:19 and 19:17] be gathered together. [Armageddon, the Day of the Lord] [29] Immediately after the tribulation of those days shall the sun be darkened, and the moon shall not give her light, and the stars shall fall from heaven, and the powers of the heavens shall be shaken: [30] And then **shall appear the sign of the Son of man in heaven:** and then shall all the tribes of the earth mourn [the Day of Atonement will address all tribes, both Jew and Gentile], and **they shall see the Son of man coming in the clouds of heaven with power and great glory.** [31] And he shall send his angels with a great sound of a trumpet, and they shall gather together his elect from the four winds, from one end of heaven to the other. [i.e. the rapture, the parallel passage being Mark 13:27, where the elect are also gathered from the "uttermost part of the earth."]

### Revelation 1:7

*Behold, he cometh with clouds; and **every eye shall see him**, and they also which pierced him* [reference Zechariah 12:10]: *and **all kindreds*** [the tribes of Matthew 24:30] *of the earth shall wail because of him* [the Day of Atonement]. *Even so, Amen.*

### Revelation 19:11-14

*And **I saw heaven opened**, and behold a white horse; and he that sat upon him was called Faithful and True, and in righteousness he doth judge and make war.* [12] *His eyes were as a flame of fire, and on his head were many crowns; and he had a name written, that no man knew, but he himself.* [13] *And he was clothed with a vesture dipped in blood: and his name is called The Word of God.* [14] *And the armies which were in heaven followed him upon white horses, clothed in fine linen, white and clean* [the previously raptured Bride of Christ].

Thus, it is apparent that unbelieving Gentiles who do not take the mark of the beast will see Jesus, have the opportunity to repent, and accept Him the same way the Jews who survive the Tribulation will accept Him. And then, with respect to the Jews, Paul's words from Romans 11:26 - that "all Israel shall be saved" – will come true.

"How can this be?" pre-Tribbers will ask, since Revelation seems to indicate that the entire Gentile world, every person in it, will either be a believer marked by the antichrist for death or an unbeliever who takes his mark. The reality is, Scripture nowhere says that the antichrist will have control of every single person on the earth. There are over seven billion people on the earth, and many of the people groups that comprise the earth's population are in remote corners of the world. The antichrist will be a political, financial, and military beast who will have little concern for people groups who participate only marginally in those realms. These people groups will pose no threat to him, and it is a safe bet that he will spend precious little time trying to track down every Gabi Gabi in Australia, every Pirahã in the Brazilian Amazon, every Qechua in the Bolivian Altiplano, every Sami in Nordic countries, every Uyghur in China, every Bedouin in the wilderness of Jordan, and on and on and on, to force his mark upon them. Christians have a tendency to hyper-sensationalize the antichrist because of the hyperbole and apocalyptic language of Revelation, but he will be functioning within the normal constraints of geopolitics and global finance. Thus, passages such as…

### Revelation 13:7-8, 16-17

*And it was given unto him to make war with the saints, and to overcome them: and power was given him over all kindreds, and tongues, and nations* [i.e., types of people, not every person]. *⁸ And all that dwell upon the earth shall worship him, whose names are not written in the book of life of the Lamb slain from the foundation of the world. ¹⁶ And he causeth all [i.e., types of people], both small and great, rich and poor, free and bond, to receive a mark in their right hand, or in their foreheads: ¹⁷ And that no man might buy or sell, save he that had the mark, or the name of the beast, or the number of his name.*

...seem to be all-encompassing. But there is a limit placed, for certainly those whose names *are* "written in the book of life of the Lamb slain from the foundation of the world" will not worship him, receive his mark, or participate in trade or commerce with his system. The use of the terms "buy or sell" indicates those who are involved in conventional trade and commerce. Remote people groups mostly are not involved with such things and still function as hunter-gatherers, herders, and trader-barterers. Jews who flee to the wilderness of Jordan during the Tribulation and Christians hiding from the antichrist in various parts of the globe will not be participating in his global economic and religious systems, so why would it be difficult to understand that remote, non-Christian groups also will not participate in these systems? The point of all this is to say that there will be people groups who survive the Tribulation, are saved near the end of it during Trumpets and Atonement, and then move into Christ's millennial kingdom to repopulate the earth. It is these people who are described in Matthew 24 and Luke 17.

## Matthew 24:37-41

*But as the days of Noah were, so shall also the coming of the Son of man be. ³⁸ For as in the days that were before the flood they were eating and drinking, marrying and giving in marriage, until the day that Noe entered into the ark, ³⁹ And knew not until the flood came, and took them all away; so shall also the coming of the Son of man be. ⁴⁰ Then shall two be in the field; the one shall be taken, **and the other left**. ⁴¹ Two women shall be grinding at the mill; the one shall be taken, **and the other left**.*

## Luke 17:26, 33-37

*And as it was in the days of Noe, so shall it be also in the days of the Son of man. ³³ Whosoever shall seek to save his life shall lose it; and whosoever shall lose his life shall preserve it. ³⁴ I tell you, in that night there shall be two men in one bed; the one shall be taken, and **the other shall be left**. ³⁵ Two women shall be grinding together; the one shall be taken, and **the other left**. ³⁶ Two men shall be in the field; the one shall be taken, and **the other left**. ³⁷ And they answered and said unto him, Where, Lord? And he said unto them, Wheresoever the body is, thither will the eagles be gathered together* [at the Valley of Megiddo, the winepress of God's wrath].

These passages have been misinterpreted by pre-Tribbers as pertaining to the rapture; they believe that those who are taken are the elect and those left behind are the non-elect who will have to endure the Tribulation. It is quite the opposite. Consider the "days of Noah." Noah and his family were those who were "left behind" to repopulate the earth. In contrast, as Matthew states it, the lost souls of Noah's time were engaging in riotous living until the flood "took them all away," meaning they were removed from the land of the living. Those who will be engaging in riotous living at the time of Christ's return also will, in like manner, be taken from the land of the living by being taken to the Valley of Megiddo, or Armageddon, where Jesus will gather all flesh to trample them as if He were walking on grapes in a winepress. As Jesus answered the disciples regarding where the men and women of Luke 17:34-36 will be taken, He made it clear it will be a place where birds of prey will feast.

### Isaiah 63:1-6

*Who is this that cometh from Edom, with dyed garments from Bozrah?* [modern Jordan, where the Jews will be hiding during the Tribulation] *this that is glorious in his apparel, travelling in the greatness of his strength? I that speak in righteousness, mighty to save.* <sup>2</sup> *Wherefore art thou red in thine apparel, and thy garments like him that treadeth in the **winefat**?* <sup>3</sup> *I have trodden the **winepress** alone; and of the people there was none with me: for I will tread them in mine anger, and trample them in my fury; and their blood shall be sprinkled upon my* *garments, and I will stain all my raiment.* ⁴ *For the **day of vengeance** is in mine heart, and the year of my redeemed is come.* ⁵ *And I looked, and there was none to help; and I wondered that there was none to uphold: therefore mine own arm brought salvation unto me; and my fury, it upheld me.* ⁶ *And I will tread down the people in mine anger, and make them drunk in my fury, and I will bring down their strength to the earth.*

## Joel 3:1-2, 11-15

*For, behold, in those days, and in that time, when I shall bring again the captivity of Judah and Jerusalem,* ² *I will also gather all nations, and will bring them down into the valley of Jehoshaphat* [another name for Megiddo, used to show comparability to Jehoshaphat's miraculous victory over the Moabites and Ammonites through God's direct intervention, described in 2 Chronicles 20] *and will plead with them there for my people and for my heritage Israel, whom they have scattered among the nations, and parted my land.* ¹¹ *Assemble yourselves, and come, all ye heathen, and gather yourselves together round about: thither cause thy mighty ones to come down, O LORD.* ¹² *Let the heathen be wakened, and come up to the valley of Jehoshaphat: for there will I sit to judge all the heathen round about.* ¹³ **Put ye in the sickle, for the harvest is ripe: come, get you down; for the press is full, the fats overflow;** *for their* *wickedness is great.* <sup>14</sup>*Multitudes, multitudes in the valley of decision: for the day of the* LORD *is near in the valley of decision.* <sup>15</sup>*The sun and the moon shall be darkened, and the stars shall withdraw their shining.*

## Revelation 14:14-20

*And I looked, and behold a white cloud, and upon the cloud one sat like unto the Son of man* [Jesus]*, having on his head a golden crown, and in his hand a **sharp sickle**.* <sup>15</sup>*And another angel came out of the temple, crying with a loud voice to him that sat on the cloud, Thrust in thy sickle, and reap: for the time is come for thee to reap; for the harvest of the earth is ripe.* <sup>16</sup>*And he that sat on the cloud thrust in his sickle on the earth; and the earth was reaped.* [This is the rapture, the harvest of the wheat mentioned in Matthew 13:30.] <sup>17</sup>*And another angel came out of the temple which is in heaven, he also having a **sharp sickle**.* <sup>18</sup>*And another angel came out from the altar, which had power over fire; and cried with a loud cry to him that had the **sharp sickle**, saying, Thrust in thy **sharp sickle**, and gather the **clusters of the vine of the earth**; for her **grapes** are fully ripe.* <sup>19</sup>*And the angel thrust in his sickle into the earth, and gathered the vine of the earth, and cast it into the great **winepress of the wrath of God**.* [This is the gathering of the antichrist's followers for wrath at Armageddon, i.e., the removal of the tares mentioned in Matthew 13:30.] *²⁰ And the winepress was trodden without the city, and blood came out of the winepress, even unto the horse bridles, by the space of a thousand and six hundred furlongs.*

### Revelation 19:17-18

*And I saw an angel standing in the sun; and he* cried with a loud voice, saying to all the **fowls** [the same fowls as those of Luke 17:37] *that fly in the midst of heaven, Come and gather yourselves together unto the supper of the great God* [This is at the winepress, the Valley of Armageddon.]; *¹⁸ That ye may eat the flesh of kings, and the flesh of captains, and the flesh of mighty men, and the flesh of horses, and of them that sit on them, and the flesh of all men, both free and bond, both small and great.* [Note that this immediately follows the introduction of the Bride, consistent with the idea of the rapture followed closely by the Day of the Lord.]

What the Lord will do to those who are taken to the winepress will be utterly horrific.

### Zechariah 14:12

*And this shall be the plague wherewith the LORD will smite all the people that have fought against Jerusalem; Their flesh shall consume away while*

74

*they stand upon their feet, and their eyes shall consume away in their holes, and their tongue shall consume away in their mouth.*

Those who are left behind are those who will recognize Jesus for who He is, repent, and enter the millennial kingdom. In other words, the ones who are taken are those who are harvested by the second sickle of Revelation 14:19, taken to the "valley of decision," - which is Armageddon - and trampled by Jesus in the valley "winepress"; those who are left behind will be both Jews and Gentiles who repent before or on the Day of Atonement and then enter into the thousand years of rest under Christ's direct rule on the earth.

Observe that the timing of the two harvests of Revelation 14:14-20 are back-to-back and immediately before the destruction of the godless "grapes." This fits our narrative precisely: Trumpets (rapture), followed closely by the Day of the Lord. It also corresponds to the end-times harvest of the wheat and the tares at "the end of the world":

### Matthew 13:37-40

*He answered and said unto them, He that soweth the good seed is the Son of man; [38] The field is the world; the good seed are the children of the kingdom; but the tares are the children of the wicked one; [39] The enemy that sowed them is the devil; **the harvest is the end of the world**; and the reapers are the angels. [40] As therefore the tares are gathered and burned in the fire; so shall it be in the end of this world.*

So, to sum it up, here is the chain of events described by the last three feasts of Israel:

> 1. Trumpets (Tishri 1, September/October) – a holy convocation, a gathering of God's people, the first sickle harvest of Revelation 14:14-20, "the rapture." This begins the ten Days of Awe wherein the as-yet-unsaved elect destined for salvation will begin introspection and serious consideration of recent events to prepare their hearts for the...

> 2. Day of Atonement (Tishri 10) – elect Jews and Gentiles who survive the Tribulation recognize Jesus and are saved. He will be revealed openly, as Zechariah 12:10, Matthew 24:27-31, Revelation 1:7, and Revelation 19:11-14 make clear.

Then occurs the interlude of Armageddon and the destruction of the antichrist, the false prophet, and their followers on the Day of the Lord in "the great winepress of the wrath of God," i.e., all those who take the mark of the beast; it will be the second sickle harvest of Revelation 14:14-20. Finally...

> 3. Tabernacles (Tishri 15) – Jesus triumphantly enters Jerusalem and tabernacles among His people for 1,000 years.

It is unclear to me exactly how the interludes of the days between Trumpets and Atonement and between Atonement and Tabernacles will play out, but suffice it to say that Jesus will accomplish these final feasts in the same way He accomplished the first four feasts – consecutively in the exact way they are presented on the Jewish calendar. Perhaps the Day of the Lord will occur the day after Atonement, or on the same day as the first day of Tabernacles, or perhaps the day before. I don't know. Further study and the research of others may elucidate the correct timing.

# Chapter Three
# THOSE NOISY TRUMPETS

The pre-Tribbers note that almost one hundred uses of "trumpet/trumpets" are in the OT and then caution the student of prophecy not to equate too quickly the trumpets in any two texts without significant agreement between the contexts of the verses. There are trumpets of warning; calls to gather, worship/praise, stand-down or return from battle; calls of victory, scattering, or dispersal (going back home); rejoicing; proclamation; etc. They state that of the primary passages used by post-Tribbers as proof texts, each has a trumpet used for a purpose different from the other passages. The trumpet of Joel 2:1 is a trumpet of warning that the Day of the Lord is at hand; the trumpet of 1 Thessalonians 4:16 and 1 Corinthians 15:52-53 is a trumpet which proclaims the approaching King so that people may go out to meet Him; the trumpet of Matthew 24:31 is a call to gather; and the trumpet of Revelation 11:15 is the seventh of seven announcing victory. They are adamant that there is no overwhelming reason to equate the rapture trumpet with any of the other trumpets, maintaining that these texts cannot be used to determine the timing of the rapture.

I liken that approach to muddying the waters in an attempt to obscure the post-Trib viewpoint rather than adding clarity. It is akin to using a shotgun when a sniper rifle is needed. Whereas trumpets were used for multiple purposes in the OT, nothing in Scripture precludes the blowing of *one* trumpet to have *multiple* purposes. There is nothing to preclude *one* trumpet for *warning* the inhabitants

79

of the earth to repent; *proclaiming* the return of the King; *calling* the faithful to gather; and *announcing* victory. The requisite trumpet passages specific to the rapture debate are presented below:

### Joel 2:1

*Blow ye the **trumpet** in Zion, and sound an alarm in my holy mountain: let all the inhabitants of the land tremble: for the day of the L*ORD* cometh, for it is nigh at hand;*

### Matthew 24:31

*And he shall send his angels with a great sound of a **trumpet**, and they shall gather together his elect from the four winds, from one end of heaven to the other.*

Mark further clarifies that the elect are not only gathered from heaven at the sound of the trumpet but also from earth. The totality of this gathering can only mean the rapture.

### Mark 13:27

*And then shall he send his angels, and shall gather together his elect from the four winds, **from the uttermost part of the earth to the uttermost part of heaven**.*

Continuing on with the trumpets…

### 1 Corinthians 15:51-52

*Behold, I shew you a **mystery**; We shall not all sleep, but we shall all be changed,* $^{52}$ *In a moment, in the twinkling of an eye, **at the last trump**:* [the 7th trumpet sounding by the 7th angel of Revelation 11:15] *for the trumpet shall sound, and the dead shall be raised incorruptible, and we shall be changed* [i.e., the rapture].

### 1 Thessalonians 4:16

*For the Lord himself shall descend from heaven with a shout, with the voice of the archangel, and with the **trump** of God: and the dead in Christ shall rise first:*

### Revelation 10:7

*But in the days of the voice of the **seventh** angel* [the last one, as mentioned by Paul in 1 Corinthians 15:52, i.e., the rapture], *when he shall begin to **sound*** [his trumpet], *the **mystery** of God should be finished* [the same mystery as mentioned by Paul in 1 Corinthians 15:51, i.e., the rapture], *as he hath declared to his servants the prophets.*

## Revelation 11:15-19

*And the **seventh** angel sounded* [the 7th and last trumpet, the same one as in 1 Corinthians 15:52]; *and there were great voices in heaven, saying, The kingdoms of this world are become the kingdoms of our Lord, and of his Christ; and he shall reign for ever and ever.* 16 *And the four and twenty elders, which sat before God on their seats, fell upon their faces, and worshipped God,* 17 *Saying, We give thee thanks, O LORD God Almighty, which art, and wast, and art to come; because thou hast taken to thee thy great power, and hast reigned.* 18 *And the nations were angry, and thy wrath* [the Day of the Lord, the great day of His wrath from Revelation 6:17] *is come, and the time of the dead, that they should be judged, and that thou shouldest give reward* [the reward being glorified bodies at the rapture] *unto thy servants the prophets, and to the saints, and them that fear thy name, small and great; and shouldest destroy them which destroy the earth.* 19 *And the temple of God was opened in heaven, and there was seen in his temple the ark of his testament: and there were lightnings, and voices, and thunderings, and an earthquake, and great hail.*

From the general principle stated in Appendix B that Scripture unlocks and supports Scripture, these passages equate the timing of the last trumpet of Revelation - meaning the end of the Tribulation - with the revealing of the mystery, that mystery being the rapture. It is clear that the mystery, i.e., the rapture, is at the end of the Tribulation - a post-Trib rapture, if you will.

More needs to be said to address the shotgun approach of the Pre-Trib position that states that the trumpets can mean any number of things not necessarily related to the rapture. Joel 2:1 places the trumpet with the Day of the Lord. There is nothing left of the old, pagan system under the antichrist after the Day of the Lord. A thorough analysis of the 48 passages where it is mentioned makes it clear that there is finality to it. Consider Zephaniah 1:18, where "...he shall make even a speedy riddance of all them that dwell in the land." Therefore, the Joel 2:1 trumpet is *the last trumpet*.

Matthew 24:41 and Mark 13:27 state that the elect are gathered from heaven and earth. This can be nothing other than the rapture, and 1 Corinthians 15:51-52 say the rapture is a mystery and that this mystery is at *the last trumpet*. Revelation 10:7 says the mystery will be finished at the seventh - meaning last - trumpet. Revelation 11:15-19 say the last trumpet announces God's wrath, which is the Day of the Lord, which takes us back to Joel 2:1, which says the Day of the Lord is announced with a trumpet. One nice, circular, complete package that teaches the trumpet calling for the elect is the same one announcing the returning King at *the end of the Tribulation*.

# Chapter Four
# WHAT ABOUT THE RESTRAINER?

Pre-Tribbers maintain that proof of a pre-Trib rapture can be found in 2 Thessalonians 2:7.

### 2 Thessalonians 2:1-9

*Now we beseech you, brethren, by the coming of our Lord Jesus Christ, and by our gathering together unto him,* ² *That ye be not soon shaken in mind, or be troubled, neither by spirit, nor by word, nor by letter as from us, as that the day of Christ is at hand.* ³ *Let no man deceive you by any means: for that day shall not come, except there come a falling away first, and that man of sin be revealed, the son of perdition;* ⁴ *Who opposeth and exalteth himself above all that is called God, or that is worshipped; so that he as God sitteth in the temple of God, shewing himself that he is God.* ⁵ *Remember ye not, that, when I was yet with you, I told you these things?* ⁶ *And now ye know what withholdeth that he might be revealed in his time.* ⁷ *For the mystery of iniquity doth already work: only he who now letteth* [from Old English "lettan," meaning to restrain, obstruct, or hinder] *will let* [restrain, obstruct, or hinder], *until he be taken out of the way.* ⁸ *And then shall that Wicked be revealed, whom the Lord shall consume with the spirit of his mouth, and shall*

*destroy with the brightness of his coming: ⁹ Even*
*him, whose coming is after the working of Satan*
*with all power and signs and lying wonders,*

Their position is that the Holy Spirit restrains the appearance of the antichrist, so that if the Holy Spirit is "taken out of the way," then it signifies the removal of the Church via the rapture, since the Holy Spirit lives in the Church. But Scripture "cannot be broken," as Jesus said, nor can it contradict itself, though it may seem to us that it does at times. To believe the pre-Trib rapture interpretation of 2 Thessalonians 2:7, one must ignore the following passages, or at least terribly contort their straight-forward meaning:

**Psalm 139:7-12**

*Whither shall I go from **thy spirit**? or whither*
*shall I flee from thy presence? ⁸ If I ascend up into*
*heaven, thou art there: if I make my bed in hell,*
*behold, thou art there. ⁹ If I take the wings of the*
*morning, and dwell in the uttermost parts of the*
*sea; ¹⁰ Even there shall thy hand lead me, and thy*
*right hand shall hold me. ¹¹ If I say, Surely the*
*darkness shall cover me; even the night shall be*
*light about me. ¹² Yea, the darkness hideth not*
*from thee; but the night shineth as the day: the*
*darkness and the light are both alike to thee.*

### Matthew 28:20

*Teaching them to observe all things whatsoever I have commanded you: and, lo, I am with you always, even unto the end of the world. Amen.*

### John 14:16

*And I will pray the Father, and he shall give you another Comforter, that he may abide with you for ever;*

### John 15:26

*But when the Comforter is come, whom I will send unto you from the Father, even the Spirit of truth, which proceedeth from the Father, he shall testify of me:*

### John 16:13

*Howbeit when he, the Spirit of truth, is come, he will guide you into all truth: for he shall not speak of himself; but whatsoever he shall hear, that shall he speak: and he will shew you things to come.*

The pre-Tribbers freely acknowledge that there will be converts to the faith during the Tribulation. They say many will come to Christ after their loved ones and friends are suddenly raptured, perhaps because they remember the gospel preached to them before or perhaps as a result of the evangelizing being conducted by the 144,000 sealed Jews of Revelation 7 and 14. But will the Holy Spirit be less inclined to inhabit planet earth during the Tribulation than He was to inhabit hell during the time of the psalmist, King David (Psalm 139:7-12)? No! Will these Tribulation believers receive Christ by any other means than that by which the rest of us received Him? No! They will be wooed by the Spirit through His testifying and baptized into the Body of Christ by that same Spirit, and that same Spirit will be the one sustaining them and leading them "into all truth," as Jesus promised every other believer. Therefore, using a supposition to state that the Holy Spirit is the restrainer of 2 Thessalonians 2:7, and that His alleged removal means we will be raptured before the Tribulation, is reading into the passage (eisegesis), not reading out of it (exegesis).

There are strong arguments to be made that the things being withheld (Greek *katechón*) of verse 6 and the things being restrained (Greek *katechōn*) of verse 7 are the apostasy and the rising up of the antichrist from the midst of humanity. Until these two things happen and are no longer withheld or restrained, he will not be revealed for who he truly is, the Wicked (one) of 2 Thessalonians 2:8. Until that Wicked is revealed, Paul clearly states in verse 2 that the "day of Christ" will not occur, and he clearly links the "day of Christ" to the coming of the Lord and our gathering together to Him in verse 1. The coming of the Lord and our gathering together to Him is the rapture, and it occurs after the revealing of the antichrist.

Were one still to insist that the restrainer has to be a person, then I suggest that the Archangel Michael might be a good candidate. This idea is not my own and has been postulated by other students of prophecy, so I think it is worthy of mention. The basis for this theory is that Michael is presented prominently as a protector of Israel and also Satan's opponent in Daniel 10:13,21 and 12:1; Jude 1:9; and Revelation 12:7. Perhaps God tells Michael to stand down and let Satan have his way for a time before God tells him to swoop in and toss that rapscallion into the fiery brink. The postulation of Michael as the restrainer is certainly more supportable and less in violation of Scripture regarding the nature and ministry of the Holy Spirit than the postulation of the Holy Spirit as the restrainer.

To those who want to explore the restrainer, the hinderer, the obstructer further, I would recommend the following websites:

http://www.bibletruth.cc/the_restrainer.htm

http://www.logosapostolic.org/bible_study/RP355-9-2Thessalonians2v7.htm

In summation, a pre-Trib rapture cannot be argued on the basis of the rapture being equated to the removal of the Holy Spirit from the earth through removal of the Church to allow the antichrist to be revealed. It violates the basic theologies of the omnipresence of the Spirit; His ministry to all believers at all times in all places; and the timing of the rapture at the end of the Tribulation, as demonstrated by the exegesis of the passages on the feasts and trumpets and, in the following chapter, imminence.

## Chapter Five
# THE IMMINENCE ISSUE

The imminence issue relates to the belief held by pre-Tribbers that a post-Trib rapture is not possible because Christ's Second Coming will be very noticeable and will be predictable, based on counting the days from the middle of the 7-year covenant of Daniel 9:27, or alternately from the time that the antichrist declares himself to be God. Since Revelation gives us the timing of Christ's return and the destruction of the antichrist as 3.5 years or 1,260 days or 42 months after this event, the argument is that Jesus could not be referring to His Second Coming when He and the apostles spoke of it in terms of it being like a thief that could catch us off guard. In other words, the return of Christ, i.e., the rapture from the pre-Trib perspective, is imminent and could happen anytime without any specific, prescribed events to warn us of its timing.

### Matthew 24:36, 42-44

*But of that day and hour knoweth no man, no, not the angels of heaven, but my Father only. ⁴² Watch therefore: for ye know not what hour your Lord doth come. ⁴³ But know this, that if the goodman of the house had known in what watch the **thief** would come, he would have watched, and would not have suffered his house to be broken up. ⁴⁴ Therefore be ye also ready: for in such an hour as ye think not the Son of man cometh.*

## 1 Thessalonians 5:1-9

*But of the times and the seasons, brethren, ye have no need that I write unto you. ² For yourselves know perfectly that the day of the Lord so cometh as a **thief** in the night. ³ For when they shall say, Peace and safety; then sudden destruction cometh upon them, as travail upon a woman with child; and they shall not escape. ⁴ But ye, brethren, are not in darkness, that that day should overtake you as a **thief**. ⁵ Ye are all the children of light, and the children of the day: we are not of the night, nor of darkness. ⁶ Therefore let us not sleep, as do others; but let us watch and be sober. ⁷ For they that sleep sleep in the night; and they that be drunken are drunken in the night. ⁸ But let us, who are of the day, be sober, putting on the breastplate of faith and love; and for an helmet, the hope of salvation. ⁹ For God hath not appointed us to wrath, but to obtain salvation by our Lord Jesus Christ,*

## 2 Peter 3:10

*But the day of the Lord will come as a **thief** in the night; in the which the heavens shall pass away with a great noise, and the elements shall melt with fervent heat, the earth also and the works that are therein shall be burned up.*

Therefore, the pre-Trib position states that Jesus, Paul, and Peter teach that the timing of the rapture cannot be known; thus, it must be a secret gathering before His return.

Nothing could be further from the truth. In Matthew 24:36, Jesus says that only the day and hour cannot be known, but He implies the general timeframe can be known to one who is watchful. In any case, He limited the lack of knowing to only a day and an hour, not to lengthy periods, suggesting we can generally know in which watch He is coming. Even then, He was speaking in the past of a truth that was true for Him at that time; He did not apply it to His future, glorified state.

We need to bear in mind that, as God, Jesus will be the One returning and will have to know when He is returning. As Revelation 1:1 proclaims, the revelation of end-times events was given to Jesus by the Father to show us, His servants, things to come:

### Revelation 1:1

*The Revelation of Jesus Christ, which God gave unto him, to shew unto his servants things which must shortly come to pass; and he sent and signified it by his angel unto his servant John:*

How in the world can anyone continue to use Matthew 24:36, 42-44 to propagate a pre-Trib rapture position based on the imminence teaching after reading Revelation 1:1? The verse clearly says that Jesus has knowledge of the events of the future; He has to, since He will be the One orchestrating these events. Jesus is in His glorified body and no longer under the constraints of His human body. There are several examples in the NT where Jesus in His human form did not know about a certain issue and asked other people to gain information.

- Mark 5:25-34 – The hemorrhagic woman who touched His clothes

- Mark 6:34-38 – The feeding of the 5,000

- Mark 9:17-27 – The boy who was exorcised of a demon of muteness

Scripture teaches that the Spirit was given to Him without measure, meaning that, as our example, He was totally under the control of the Holy Spirit; and the Spirit revealed to Jesus only what the Spirit chose to reveal. Scripture teaches that He experienced what we experience.

### Hebrews 4:15

*For we have not an high priest which cannot be touched with the feeling of our infirmities; but was in all points tempted like as we are, yet without sin.*

Certainly, Jesus in His human body lacked knowledge of the exact timing of His return, but to extrapolate Matthew 24:36 to an all-encompassing theology that a pre-Trib rapture is taught in that verse violates too many other passages about

Christ in His glorified, omniscient state and the verb tense of the verse itself.

With respect to Paul, he was telling the Thessalonian believers that the "thief in the night" phenomenon applies only to unbelievers. He told them that that day of wrath, the "day of the Lord," would not overtake them because they were children of light. It is only that particular day that Paul was saying would not overtake them; he did not say that they would sit out the entire Tribulation. Since Paul did not know when all the events leading up to the return of Christ would occur, and since Paul knew of the Lord's admonition to be watching at all times, he was well within reason to speak to the Thessalonians as if these things could happen in their lifetimes.

Paul told the Thessalonians that the Day of the Lord would not overtake them, but it will not be the case for the unsaved; they will be caught off guard by the return of Christ. That being said, the imminence doctrine of the pre-Trib position does not apply to believers but only to unbelievers. Paul contrasts the believers who are of the light, sober, and watchful to unbelievers who are in darkness, drunken, and sleepy. To the latter people, the return of Christ most assuredly will be unexpected.

We see this idea again in Hebrews 10:25, in which Paul exhorts the believers to stick together even more, since they "see **the day** [of the Lord's return] approaching." If Paul were a pre-Tribber, why would he feel compelled to urge Christians to maintain fellowship even more than normal if he knew they would be extracted out of this world to sit the Tribulation out in heaven? He would not. Seen from a post-Trib perspective, this verse makes total sense. Paul knew that

Christians would be right in the thick of the Tribulation, undergoing great persecution and travail, such that sticking together would be all the more important for support and comfort.

Paul knew that the true source of comfort to the believers undergoing tribulation would be the return of Christ. You can see this idea again in his second letter to the Thessalonians. The rest from tribulation will be when "the Lord Jesus shall be revealed from heaven," not when a secret rapture at some mysterious, unpredictable time occurs. In fact, Paul mentions the tribulation that the Thessalonians were undergoing and says that those who were troubling the Thessalonians would themselves undergo tribulation. This is a model for how it will occur to the last-days Church. The timing of the rapture, the *rest*, is therefore linked to the timing of the Day of the Lord. They are essentially in one short period with several steps.

### 2 Thessalonians 1:6-10

*Seeing it is a righteous thing with God to recompense tribulation to them that trouble you; 7 And to you who are troubled **rest** with us, when the Lord Jesus shall be revealed from heaven with his mighty angels, 8 In flaming fire taking vengeance on them that know not God, and that obey not the gospel of our Lord Jesus Christ: 9 Who shall be punished with everlasting destruction from the presence of the Lord, and from the glory of his power; 10 When he shall come to be glorified in his saints, and to be admired in all them that* *believe (because our testimony among you was believed) in that day.*

The idea of comfort and its connection to resurrection and, therefore, the rapture, is seen in Martha's dialog with Jesus regarding her dead brother, Lazarus. Note that Lazarus "shall *rise* again in the resurrection at the last day," reminiscent of Paul's assertion in 1 Thessalonians 4:16 that "the dead in Christ shall *rise* first." In common vernacular, when someone uses the word "last," we recognize it as meaning at the end of something, not before or at the beginning.

### John 11:20-24

*Then Martha, as soon as she heard that Jesus was coming, went and met him: but Mary sat still in the house.* <sup>21</sup> *Then said Martha unto Jesus, Lord, if thou hadst been here, my brother had not died.* <sup>22</sup> *But I know, that even now, whatsoever thou wilt ask of God, God will give it thee.* <sup>23</sup> *Jesus saith unto her, Thy brother shall rise again.* <sup>24</sup> *Martha saith unto him, I know that he shall rise again in the resurrection* [the rapture] *at the **last day**.*

Therefore, the imminence issue is solved without violating Scripture. Yes, we can satisfy a post-Trib view that the timing of the rapture can be generally known to those believers enduring the Tribulation, which will give them hope and strength to "endureth to the end," (Matthew 10:22); and yes, we can satisfy a pre-Trib view that the timing of the rapture cannot be generally known, but it only applies to unbelievers, those of the darkness of night who are drunk and asleep.

# Chapter Six
# IN SUMMATION

We have defined the major points of the eschatology of the majority of Western, evangelical Christians, specifically the following:

1.  A man with global influence - termed in the Bible the antichrist - will come onto the world scene sometime in the future and make a 7-year covenant with Israel. This covenant will result in many things, but specifically it will allow the rebuilding of a temple comparable to the one the Israelites had in their 40-year wilderness wanderings.

2.  In the middle of that 7-year covenant, the antichrist will break the covenant with Israel and declare himself to be God. The Jews in Israel will flee to the wilderness of Jordan. The latter half of the 7-year period will be the Tribulation. The world will suffer great economic, political, social, religious, and physical upheaval, with wars, earthquakes, famines, and disease leading to massive human death. Sometime before, during, or at the end of the Tribulation, the Church will be caught up, "raptured," to meet Jesus and be given glorified, immortal bodies.

3.  At the end of the Tribulation, Jesus will gather the antichrist and his followers to the Valley of Armageddon, where Jesus will destroy them all during the Day of the Lord. He will then enter Jerusalem and

rule for 1,000 years from a new temple built by Himself. At the end of the 1,000 years, the nations will again be deceived by Satan, resulting in their destruction by God and the establishment of the eternal New Jerusalem on earth.

The major bone of contention among the evangelicals is the timing of the rapture, whether it is pre-, mid-, or post-Trib. The two major views among these three are the pre- and post-positions. We have studied four major points of contention between these two views, specifically how to interpret the pattern of the feasts of Israel, how to interpret the trumpets that signal the rapture and Christ's return, how to interpret the restrainer, and how to interpret the imminence issue. The conclusions of these studies are as follows.

1. Jesus fulfilled the first four feasts of Israel in the same calendar year in the exact order they occur on the calendar during His first advent and will do it in the same manner during His second advent. The last three feasts consist of Trumpets, which is the rapture; then Atonement, where the survivors of the Tribulation will have the final opportunity to repent; and finally Tabernacles, when Jesus will set up His millennial kingdom. These feasts will occur over a 15-day period *at the end of the Tribulation*, i.e., a post-Trib rapture.

2. The trumpets mentioned in Joel, 1 Thessalonians, 1 Corinthians, and Revelation are the seventh and last trumpet of the Tribulation period. Paul says in 1 Corinthians that the rapture is a mystery, and John in

Revelation says that the mystery will be finished at the last trumpet. The rapture is distinctly associated with this seventh and last trumpet, meaning the rapture is a post-Trib rapture.

3. The restrainer of 2 Thessalonians 2:7 which must be "taken out of the way" to permit the rapture cannot be the Holy Spirit, since it violates other Scripture that says He is omnipresent and will always be with believers. This verse cannot be used to teach a pre-Trib rapture by stating that the Church will be raptured when the Holy Spirit is taken out of the way before the antichrist's ascent. Perhaps the Archangel Michael is the restrainer by virtue of his position as Israel's chief, angelic protector; at least he is a better candidate for the restrainer than the Holy Spirit. However, it is more likely that the restraining things that must be permitted to occur to allow the rapture are the apostasy and the revelation of the antichrist. The apostasy and the antichrist's reign occur during the Tribulation, and the rapture is *after* these things, meaning a post-Trib rapture.

4. The imminent return of Jesus cannot be understood as an argument for a pre-Trib rapture. The imminence issue applies only to those who are not looking for Him, namely the lost. In 1 Thessalonians 5, Paul tells the believers that they (and also we) are children of the light and will not be caught unaware by the Day of the Lord and will not suffer God's wrath. The Day of the Lord is one day, not the entire Tribulation. The Tribulation is a time of judgments, not wrath, to allow

101

repentance and the revealing of the attributes of God, but the Day of the Lord is a day of wrath and utter destruction. Therefore, Paul is telling them in 1 Thessalonians 4 and 5 that the Church will not experience the wrath of God demonstrated on the Day of the Lord at the end of the Tribulation and will be caught up, i.e., raptured, meaning a post-Trib rapture. It is only this one day to which believers have not been "appointed," as Paul told the Thessalonians.

Other points supporting the post-Trib view are enumerated below:

1. Those taken and those left behind have been misinterpreted by pre-Tribbers. Those taken are the antichrist's followers who will be taken to the Valley of Megiddo and destroyed by Jesus on the Day of the Lord. Those left behind will be those, like Noah, who will remain to repopulate the earth during Christ's millennial kingdom.

2. Certain remote, Gentile non-believers will not follow the antichrist during the Tribulation and will survive until Trumpets and Atonement when, sometime during the Days of Awe from Trumpets to Atonement, they will accept Christ and survive to repopulate the earth during Christ's millennial kingdom.

3. The rapture is a resurrection, not a revivification or resuscitation, and there is only one resurrection in Scripture that captures the entire Body of believers at one time. It is discussed throughout the gospels and epistles, but it is illuminated in Revelation 20:6 and applies to those who will not taste of the second death, i.e., the Lake of Fire. Revelation 20:4 says that participants in this first resurrection will include those who go through the Tribulation, meaning this resurrection occurs at the end of the Tribulation. Martha told Jesus she knew this resurrection would occur on "the last day," another indicator of the rapture's post-Trib timing.

4. The two reapings of Revelation 14:14-20 are back-to-back within the Tribulation and are consistent with the timing presented herein, specifically the first reaping - the rapture – followed by the second reaping - the Day of the Lord, a.k.a. Armageddon, the Valley of Jehoshaphat, the Valley of Megiddo, the great winepress of the fierce wrath of God.

5. The elect are all believers - both before Christ's first advent and after His first advent - and they will be gathered from the ends of heaven and earth "after the Tribulation of those days," as Jesus makes clear. The gathering from the heavens include the dead in Christ who will rise first, and the gathering from the earth includes those who are alive and remain until the coming of the Lord. This is the rapture, and it is after the Tribulation.

6. Jesus said that believers who endure to the end shall be saved. Paul told the audience of Hebrews to stick together as believers even more as the day of the Lord's return approaches, indicating he knew it would get tougher for believers, with no suggestion of an "out" through a pre-Trib rapture. Paul said rest for the Thessalonians and other Christians would come when the Lord is **revealed** with His mighty angels, not when a secret, unseeable rapture occurs. The collective history of the elect, whether OT or NT saints, has been one of going **through** tribulation, not avoiding it through some type of escape. The children of Israel in the wilderness wanderings are presented by Paul as an example for those of us "upon whom the ends of world are come," and those Israelites went through tribulation on their way to the Promised Land. It will be no different for us.

# Chapter Seven
# EPILOGUE

Some final comments are in order with respect to the differences between the arguments for or against the pre-Trib and post-Trib perspectives, respectively. I was once an ardent follower of the pre-Trib position from the age of 12, when I first started studying the topic. I became more entrenched in my view when I was 17 after reading *The Late, Great Planet Earth*. I devoured many other writings of men and women of God who were excited about prophecy and who also got other Christians excited about it. All these laborers have been evangelistically and apologetically minded, and I am grateful for the positive effect they have had on the Body. And so it was for many years that I considered only their positions regarding the timing of the rapture.

It was not until Pat, a friend of mine, challenged some of my suppositions about the rapture that I embarked on an intense study at the age of 30 to nail it down for myself. That was the crux of the issue; I had been holding to my pre-Trib position based on suppositions, such as the one discussed in a previous chapter regarding the restrainer. I *supposed* that we will be raptured before the Tribulation based on the supposition that the restrainer is the Holy Spirit, and I *supposed* that removing the Holy Spirit removes us. *But the text of 2 Thessalonians 2 doesn't state that.*

And thus it is with much of the pre-Trib compendium of arguments, as I have come to see it – suppositions based on deductive reasoning, or if/then hypotheses used to support certain interpretations of passages when the relevant passages do not unequivocally state what the pre-Trib proponent is arguing. In contrast, I see the post-Trib position based more on actual statements of the timing of the rapture and connection of key words or concepts in key passages to those same key words or concepts in other key passages. Examination of...

### Mark 13:24-27

*But in those days, after that tribulation, the sun shall be darkened, and the moon shall not give her light, 25 And the stars of heaven shall fall, and the powers that are in heaven shall be shaken. 26 And then shall they see the Son of man coming in the clouds with great power and glory. 27 And then shall he send his angels, and shall gather together his elect from the four winds, from the uttermost part of the earth to the uttermost part of heaven.*

...indicates a direct statement regarding the timing of the rapture: "...**after that tribulation**...And then shall he send his angels, and shall gather together his elect from the four winds, from the uttermost part of the earth to the uttermost part of heaven."

Folks, when you gather the elect - meaning believers - from the ends of earth to the ends of heaven, it can mean only one thing – the rapture. "The dead in Christ shall rise first" from 1 Thessalonians 4:16 is the same thing as gathering the elect from the "four winds" of heaven from Mark 13:27. The "we which are alive and remain shall be caught up together with them in the clouds" from 1 Thessalonians 4:17 is the same thing as gathering the elect from the "four winds" of earth from that same Mark 13 verse. The gathering of the elect from heaven and earth is "after that tribulation." Very clear, very straight-forward.

There is also an argument to be made for a post-Trib rapture by observing how God has dealt with His people in the past with respect to other times of tribulation, specifically that God takes His people through the storms instead of away from them. The overwhelming pattern of history has been one of God sustaining His people through tribulation rather than taking them out of tribulation. Paul was no stranger to such tribulation:

### 1 Thessalonians 3:4

*For verily, when we were with you, we told you before that we should suffer tribulation; even as it came to pass, and ye know.*

### 2 Thessalonians 1:4

*So that we ourselves glory in you in the churches of God for your patience and faith in all your persecutions and tribulations that ye endure:*

Paul states in 1 Corinthians 10 that the things that happened to the Israelites in the wilderness were examples for us, "upon whom the ends of the world are come." (1 Corinthians 10:11) The Israelites went through great difficulty on their way to the Promised Land; they were not given a pass, nor were the countless Christians who had their own tribulations through the ages. I easily can imagine that the 1ˢᵗ century Roman Christians being fed to lions or being used as torches at Emperor Nero's parties would think it strange, perhaps offensive, that their end-times brethren would not get the opportunity to glorify God the way they did. But assuredly, Scripture indicates that their end-times brethren will glorify God the way they did:

### Revelation 12:11

*And they overcame him by the blood of the Lamb, and by the word of their testimony; and they loved not their lives unto the death.*

As a final witness to the truth of what I am saying in this book, I offer the Lord Himself. There was only one request that Jesus asked of the Father that was denied, specifically that the cup of His passion would pass Him by, but even in that, Jesus already knew the will of the Father. As for the High Priestly Prayer of John 17:1-26, there was nothing that the Father would deny the Son. As our example, Jesus prayed only within the confines of the Father's will, and we know that whatsoever Jesus would ask of the Father, it would be granted. What, then, do we make of the following?

### John 17:14-15

*I have given them thy word; and the world hath hated them, because they are not of the world, even as I am not of the world.* **¹⁵ I pray not that thou** *shouldest take them out of the world, but that thou shouldest keep them from the evil.*

We have already affirmed that Scripture cannot be broken. A pre-Trib rapture would break Scripture and would indicate a Father and Son not functioning as one, a repudiation of the Lord's assertion of unity in John 17:21-23. This, beloved brethren, cannot be.

The inevitable question I receive from Christians when they come to grips with the distinct possibility that they might live long enough to experience the Tribulation regards what they should do next. Then comes their own list of possibilities: build a bunker, move to a remote part of the country, horde supplies, buy gold and silver, stock up on weapons, etc., etc., and so on, and so on. I have no immediate answer for them. Far be it for me to take the place of the Holy Spirit or interfere with how God wants to deal with His precious babies. Jesus said the Holy Spirit, not Paul Wild, would guide the Church into "all truth," (John 16:13) so I presume that there will be truths specific to each Christian for what he or she must do to obey the Lord in times of crisis. The best I can do is to present some general principles for staying out of debt; keeping adequate provisions on hand that one should have for any emergency (fire, flood, wind, social unrest, etc.); having some form of defensive protection against hostiles; maintaining fellowship with other Christians who can help in time of need; and the like. What any Christian should do is what the Holy Spirit leads them to do. The point is – *do something. Doing something* is an act of faith based on something you know to be true but can't see - in other words, "the substance of things hoped for, the evidence

109

of things not seen." (Hebrews 11:1) James says that faith is demonstrated by *taking action* on what you know to be true. (James 2:14-26) Paul further reminds us that without faith it is impossible to please Him (Hebrews 11:6), and that anything not of faith is sin (Romans 14:23).

I am mindful of one my friends, Mike, who is very much aware of these prophetical issues and yet has stated he will continue on in effective ministry to prostitutes, pimps, and parolees in the inner city when all hell breaks loose (I meant that last bit literally). That being said, if God tells you to throw yourself into the thick of the chaos, then do it. It's far safer than being outside of His will. Think of Jonah.

My hope is that this study will cause complacent members of the Body of Christ to wake up and disabuse themselves of the notion that we will miss the Tribulation. My observations tell me that the pre-Trib rapture theology has caused considerable damage to the Church because it has largely removed the watchfulness that Paul admonished the Thessalonians to have and, through them, also us. Hosea 4:6 says that God's people are destroyed through lack of knowledge. There is no better example to use to demonstrate this truth than the pre-Trib rapture doctrine. As a collective, believers need to begin preparing for the Tribulation, doing as Paul advised in Hebrews 10:25, to assemble together and exhort one another even more. In a similar vein as what Benjamin Franklin once said, "We must, indeed, all hang together or, most assuredly, we shall all hang separately." I cannot help but think that gaining an understanding that we will go through the Tribulation will compel many Christians - certainly more than now - to become more serious about preparing spiritually, physically, and financially for the coming fire. As stated previously…

**Proverbs 22:3**

*A prudent man **foreseeth the evil**, and **hideth himself**: but the simple pass on, and are punished.*

There is nothing in this verse to say that Christians cannot find themselves among the simpletons who ignore the warnings and are punished. As I have found through experiencing the harsh repercussions of my own foolishness (even as a Christian), God does not always spare His children of the rotten fruit of their own poor sowing (Galatians 6:7). Thus, in closing, I say to my brethren, "Prepare now!"

# APPENDIX A – DAY OF THE LORD

1. Job 21:30

*That the wicked is reserved to the **day of destruction**? they shall be brought forth to the **day of wrath**.*

2. Psalm 110:5

*The Lord at thy right hand shall strike through kings in the **day of his wrath**.*

3. Proverbs 11:4

*Riches profit not in the **day of wrath**: but righteousness delivereth from death.*

4. Isaiah 2:12

*For the **day of the Lord** of hosts shall be upon every one that is proud and lofty, and upon every one that is lifted up; and he shall be brought low:*

5. Isaiah 13:6

*Howl ye; for the **day of the Lord** is at hand; it shall come as a destruction from the Almighty.*

6. Isaiah 13:9

*Behold, the **day of the Lord** cometh, cruel both with wrath and fierce anger, to lay the land desolate: and he shall destroy the sinners thereof out of it.*

7. Isaiah 13:13

*Therefore I will shake the heavens, and the earth shall remove out of her place, in the wrath of the LORD of hosts, and in the **day of his fierce anger.***

8. Isaiah 34:8

*For it is the **day of the Lord's** vengeance, and the year of recompences for the controversy of Zion.*

9. Isaiah 63:4

*For the **day of vengeance** is in mine heart, and the year of my redeemed is come.*

10. Jeremiah 46:10

*For this is the **day of the Lord God** of hosts, a **day of vengeance**, that he may avenge him of his adversaries: and the sword shall devour, and it shall be satiate and made drunk with their blood: for the Lord GOD of hosts hath a sacrifice in the north country by the river Euphrates.*

## 11. Lamentations 2:22

*Thou hast called as in a solemn **day** my terrors round about, so that in the **day of the Lord's** anger none escaped nor remained: those that I have swaddled and brought up hath mine enemy consumed.*

## 12. Ezekiel 7:19

*They shall cast their silver in the streets, and their gold shall be removed: their silver and their gold shall not be able to deliver them in the **day of the wrath of the Lord**: they shall not satisfy their souls, neither fill their bowels: because it is the stumblingblock of their iniquity.*

## 13. Ezekiel 13:5

*Ye have not gone up into the gaps, neither made up the hedge for the house of Israel to stand in the battle in the **day of the Lord**.*

## 14. Ezekiel 30:3

*For the **day** is near, even the **day of the Lord** is near, a cloudy day; it shall be the time of the heathen.*

## 15. Ezekiel 38:19

*For in my jealousy and in the **fire of my wrath** have I spoken, Surely in that **day** there shall be a great shaking in the land of Israel;*

## 16. Joel 1:15

*Alas for the day! for the **day of the Lord** is at hand, and as a destruction from the Almighty shall it come.*

## 17. Joel 2:1

*Blow ye the trumpet in Zion, and sound an alarm in my holy mountain: let all the inhabitants of the land tremble: for the **day of the Lord** cometh, for it is nigh at hand;*

## 18. Joel 2:11

*And the LORD shall utter his voice before his army: for his camp is very great: for he is strong that executeth his word: for the **day of the Lord** is great and very terrible; and who can abide it?*

## 19. Joel 2:31

*The sun shall be turned into darkness, and the moon into blood, before the great and terrible **day of the Lord** come.*

## 20. Joel 3:14

*Multitudes, multitudes in the valley of decision: for the **day of the Lord** is near in the valley of decision.*

## 21. Amos 5:18

*Woe unto you that desire the day of the LORD! to what end is it for you? the **day of the Lord** is darkness, and not light.*

## 22. Amos 5:20

*Shall not the **day of the Lord** be darkness, and not light? even very dark, and no brightness in it?*

## 23. Obadiah 1:15

*For the **day of the Lord** is near upon all the heathen: as thou hast done, it shall be done unto thee: thy reward shall return upon thine own head.*

## 24. Nahum 1:7

*The Lord is good, a strong hold in the **day of trouble**; and he knoweth them that trust in him.*

## 25. Habakkuk 3:16

*When I heard, my belly trembled; my lips quivered at the voice: rottenness entered into my bones, and I trembled in myself, that I might rest in the **day of trouble**: when he cometh up unto the people, he will invade them with his troops.*

## 26. Zephaniah 1:7

*Hold thy peace at the presence of the Lord GOD: for the **day of the Lord** is at hand: for the LORD hath prepared a sacrifice, he hath bid his guests.*

## 27. Zephaniah 1:8

*And it shall come to pass in the **day of the Lord's** sacrifice, that I will punish the princes, and the king's children, and all such as are clothed with strange apparel.*

## 28. Zephaniah 1:14

*The great **day of the Lord** is near, it is near, and hasteth greatly, even the voice of the day of the LORD: the mighty man shall cry there bitterly.*

## 29. Zephaniah 1:15

*That **day** is a **day of wrath**, a **day of** trouble and distress, a **day of** wasteness and desolation, a **day of** darkness and gloominess, a **day of** clouds and thick darkness,*

## 30. Zephaniah 1:18

*Neither their silver nor their gold shall be able to deliver them in the **day of the Lord's** wrath; but the whole land shall be devoured by the fire of his jealousy: for he shall make even a speedy riddance of all them that dwell in the land.*

## 31. Zephaniah 2:2

*Before the decree bring forth, before the day pass as the chaff, before the fierce anger of the LORD come upon you, before the **day of the Lord's** anger come upon you.*

## 32. Zephaniah 2:3

*Seek ye the LORD, all ye meek of the earth, which have wrought his judgment; seek righteousness, seek meekness: it may be ye shall be hid in the **day of the Lord's** anger.*

## 33. Zechariah 14:1

*Behold, the **day of the Lord** cometh, and thy spoil shall be divided in the midst of thee.*

## 34. Malachi 4:5

*Behold, I will send you Elijah the prophet before the coming of the great and dreadful **day of the Lord**:*

## 35. Acts 2:20

*The sun shall be turned into darkness, and the moon into blood, before the great and notable **day of the Lord** come:*

## 36. Romans 2:5

*But after thy hardness and impenitent heart treasurest up unto thyself **wrath** against the **day of wrath** and revelation of the righteous judgment of God;*

## 37. 1 Corinthians 1:8\*

*Who shall also confirm you unto the end, that ye may be blameless in the **day of our Lord Jesus Christ.***

### 38. 1 Corinthians 5:5*

*To deliver such an one unto Satan for the destruction of the flesh, that the spirit may be saved in the **day of the Lord Jesus.***

### 39. 2 Corinthians 1:14*

*As also ye have acknowledged us in part, that we are your rejoicing, even as ye also are ours in the **day of the Lord Jesus**.*

### 40. Philippians 1:6*

*Being confident of this very thing, that he which hath begun a good work in you will perform it until the **day of Jesus Christ:***

### 41. Philippians 1:10*

*That ye may approve things that are excellent; that ye may be sincere and without offence till the **day of Christ.***

### 42. 1 Thessalonians 5:2

*For yourselves know perfectly that the **day of the Lord** so cometh as a thief in the night.*

### 43. 2 Thessalonians 1:10

*When he shall come to be glorified in his saints, and to be admired in all them that believe (because our testimony among you was believed) in that **day**.*

## 44. 2 Thessalonians 2:2*

*That ye be not soon shaken in mind, or be troubled, neither by spirit, nor by word, nor by letter as from us, as that the **day of Christ** is at hand.*

## 45. 2 Thessalonians 2:3

*Let no man deceive you by any means: for that **day** shall not come, except there come a falling away first, and that man of sin be revealed, the son of perdition;*

## 46. 2 Peter 3:10

*But the **day of the Lord** will come as a thief in the night; in the which the heavens shall pass away with a great noise, and the elements shall melt with fervent heat, the earth also and the works that are therein shall be burned up.*

## 47. Hebrews 10:25

*Not forsaking the assembling of ourselves together, as the manner of some is; but exhorting one another: and so much the more, as ye see the **day** approaching.*

## 48. Revelation 6:17

*For the great **day of his wrath** is come; and who shall be able to stand?*

---

* Some commentators distinguish between "the day of the Lord" and "the day of our Lord Jesus Christ/Lord Jesus/Jesus Christ/Christ," stating that the contexts of the latter phrases are ones of hope, expectation, and reward for believers as opposed to the contexts of the former phrase as ones of wrath and destruction for unbelievers. Further study is needed to evaluate this distinction.

# APPENDIX B:
## RULES OF ENGAGEMENT (HERMENEUTICS, OR GUIDELINES FOR INTERPRETATION)

There are a lot of really great books on hermeneutics that can get very scholarly, complex, and detailed, like Mickelsen's classic, *Interpreting the Bible,* or Kaiser's *The Uses of the Old Testament in the New.* Or they can be made more consumable to the lay person, like Fee and Stuart's *How to Read the Bible for All Its Worth.* Rather than give summations of what these great books have to say, I thought it easier to summarize a few rules I have found to be tried and true through my years of studying Scripture. I used every one of them in my study of the subject of this book. They are as follows.

**1. God works in both nature and prophecy through parallels, patterns, and pre-types to teach precepts, principles, and prophecies.** A superb example of this principle is the Jewish holidays. The holidays were used by God to prepare the Jews for their Messiah's first advent. They were clueless to this for His first advent, but some of them eventually caught on:

**Exodus 34:22**

*And thou shalt observe the feast of weeks, of the firstfruits of wheat harvest, and the feast of ingathering at the year's end.*

### 1 Corinthians 15:20, 23

*But now is Christ risen from the dead, and become the firstfruits of them that slept. [23] But every man in his own order: Christ the firstfruits; afterward they that are Christ's at his coming.*

Another example is that He began things in a garden (Genesis 2:8), and He will end things in a garden (Revelation 22:1, 2). The post-flood, godless, pantheistic systems started in Mesopotamia (Genesis 11:1-9), and they will end in Mesopotamia (Zechariah 5:5-11; Revelation 18). The sun is the source of light; the moon reflects that light. The Son is the source of light; we reflect that light. The Bridegroom knows His Bride – spiritual intercourse; Adam knew Eve – sexual intercourse. Christ is the head of His Bride (His Body, Ephesians 4:15, 16); the husband is the head of his bride (his body, 1 Corinthians 11:3; Ephesians 5:28-30). God is tripartite (Father, Son, Spirit); we are tripartite (body, soul, spirit). Et cetera, et cetera, and so on, and so forth. Parallels. Patterns. Pre-types.

**2. There are no idle words in Scripture.** We tend to think that Scripture uses flourishing words or grandiose, pictorial language for hyperbolic effect, i.e., to intensify the emotion or idea that is being conveyed, without considering that there is a prophetical or theological teaching behind it. Or perhaps we spiritualize something and ignore the possibility that it has a quite literal meaning.  For instance, let's look at the following passages:

### Isaiah 28:16-17

*Therefore thus saith the Lord GOD, Behold, I lay in Zion for a foundation a stone, a tried stone, a precious corner stone, a sure foundation: he that believeth shall not make haste. [17] Judgment also will I lay to the line, and righteousness to the plummet: and the hail shall sweep away the refuge of lies, and the waters shall overflow the hiding place.*

### Matthew 24:15-21

*When ye therefore shall see the abomination of desolation, spoken of by Daniel the prophet, stand in the holy place, (whoso readeth, let him understand:) [16] Then let them which be in Judaea flee into the mountains: [17] Let him which is on the housetop not come down to take any thing out of his house: [18] Neither let him which is in the field return back to take his clothes. [19] And woe unto them that are with child, and to them that give suck in those days! [20] But pray ye that your flight be not in the winter, neither on the sabbath day: [21] For then shall be great tribulation, such as was not since the beginning of the world to this time, no, nor ever shall be.*

You might be tempted to spiritualize entirely the Isaiah passage by noting how it is used by Peter in 1 Peter 2:5-8 to equate the stone to Jesus and us to living stones that God uses to build His spiritual house. Dig a little deeper. The context of Isaiah 28 is the Day of the Lord (a consumption on the whole earth, v. 22) and the Lord's disannulment of the covenant with the antichrist that is described in Daniel 9:27. While the stone being laid in Zion may well refer to Jesus in the sense that He "is the stone the builders rejected," it also may refer to the temple that is to be rebuilt, the one of Revelation 11:1 that the antichrist will enter to declare himself as God. Theologians continue to debate on whether or not OT passages dealing with the prophetical have double meanings; I tend to side with those theologians who believe they do. The use of carpentry and construction terms (line, plummet) in Isaiah 28:17 suggests the future temple might also be referenced in addition to an allusion to Jesus. Furthermore, to an 8th century BC Jew of Isaiah's time, a reference to the corner stone would more likely bring to mind the temple rather than the Messiah. To demonstrate the importance of the corner stone of the temple to the Jewish people, one need only to read the statement of the Temple Mount Faithful in relation to their presentation on May 21, 2009, concerning the stone that they believe will function as the corner stone for the coming temple.

http://www.templemountfaithful.org/Events/jerus alemDay2009-2.htm Why is this significant? Well, whether it is a reference to the Messiah or a reference to the actual corner stone, those living in Israel who understand the significance of the temple construction, i.e., "he that believeth," will not need to "make haste" to escape Jerusalem – indeed, Israel itself - when the antichrist breaks the covenant and turns in wrath upon Israel. Rather, those people who believe in Jesus and understand his warning from Mark 14:15-21 to flee will have already escaped to safety, understanding that the covenant with the antichrist is the "covenant with death…and…agreement with hell" spoken of in Isaiah 28:18. This covenant likely will be what will allow the Jews to build the Revelation 11:1 temple.


**3. Words in Scripture have precise meanings.** It would be careless to assume that God always means a long time, maybe even a thousand years, when the word "day" is used simply because Peter said in 2 Peter 3:8 that God considers a day a thousand years and vice versa. Context is everything, so the meaning of a word in one passage of Scripture may not be the meaning that word has in another passage of Scripture; or conversely, it may very well have the same meaning between two passages. The point is that we cannot loosely assign a meaning to a word as equivalent to the meaning of another word simply because the two words have similar contexts; and conversely, we cannot fail to assign the same meaning between two passages when they do have the same meaning. This is especially true when we begin to unravel the meanings of words that have the idea of time attached to them, such words being "day," "time/times/half a time," "season," "year," "hour," and "month/months."

As I discussed earlier, these words cannot be used casually and interchangeably with reference to the duration of the Tribulation without serious study, nor can they be used in that same manner to identify crucial prophetical events; we must carefully study them to determine their precise meanings.

**4. Scripture unlocks Scripture**. An ideal set of passages to convey this concept is the following:

**Daniel 7:7-8, 19**

*After this I saw in the night visions, and behold a fourth beast, dreadful and terrible, and strong exceedingly; and it had great iron teeth: it devoured and brake in pieces, and stamped the residue with the feet of it: and it was diverse from all the beasts that were before it; and it had ten horns. ⁸ I considered the horns, and, behold, there came up among them another little horn, before whom there were three of the first horns plucked up by the roots: and, behold, in this horn were eyes like the eyes of man, and a mouth speaking great things. ¹⁹ Then I would know the truth of the fourth beast, which was diverse from all the others, exceeding dreadful, whose teeth were of iron, and his nails of brass; which devoured, brake in pieces, and stamped the residue with his feet;*

### Revelation 13:1-2

*And I stood upon the sand of the sea, and saw a beast rise up out of the sea, having seven heads and ten horns, and upon his horns ten crowns, and upon his heads the name of blasphemy. ² And the beast which I saw was like unto a leopard, and his feet were as the feet of a bear, and his mouth as the mouth of a lion: and the dragon gave him his power, and his seat, and great authority.*

The identity and timing of the fourth beast is somewhat mysterious in Daniel 7, but this beast is described more fully in the Revelation 13 passage. The Revelation 13 beast is an amalgamation of the three predecessor beasts of Daniel 7 and very clearly is shown to be the antichrist's kingdom. This is an end-times beast, indicating that the fourth beast of Daniel 7 is clearly an end-times beast.

**5. Scripture supports Scripture.** According to God's word, by the mouth of two or three witnesses a thing must be confirmed (Matthew 18:16; 2 Corinthians 13:1). Lo and behold, God ascribes to His own principles in His inspiration of Scripture. If an idea or particular theology is being presented somewhere else in Scripture, it's a safe bet that you will find support for that idea or theology elsewhere in Scripture. Sometimes the Bible will have a "weak" word in a passage that has an ambiguous meaning, or which may have variable meanings, but that "weak" word will be supported elsewhere by a "strong" word.

This concept is most evident in the theology of Jesus's immaculate conception. The following passages illustrate this point:

### Isaiah 7:14

*Therefore the Lord himself shall give you a sign; Behold, a virgin shall conceive, and bear a son, and shall call his name Immanuel.*

### Matthew 1:23

*Behold, a virgin shall be with child, and shall bring forth a son, and they shall call his name Emmanuel, which being interpreted is, God with us.*

Critics allege that the Hebrew word for virgin in Isaiah 7:14 - *"almah"* - can simply mean a young, unmarried woman, in an attempt to undermine the immaculate conception and virgin birth of Jesus. Thus, it is a weak word, but it is supported by the strong Greek word *"parthenos,"* which can only mean virgin in Matthew 1:23. So you see, Scripture supports itself by providing internal confirmation of a teaching through provision of multiple verses or passages that corroborate one another.

# Contact

To contact the author for speaking engagements
or for additional book purchases:

http://www.TheTimingOfTheRapture.com
Paul R. Wild
P.O. Box 218321
Houston, TX 77218

or

Worldwide Publishing Group
7710-T Cherry Park Dr, Ste 224
Houston, TX 77095
Phone: 713.766.4271
http://www.WorldwidePublishingGroup.com

Printed in the USA
CPSIA information can be obtained
at www.ICGtesting.com
LVHW092125141023
761116LV00020B/245/J